OIL PROGRAM INVESTMENTS

Oil
Program
Investments

Truman E. Anderson, Jr.

PETROLEUM PUBLISHING COMPANY
Tulsa

TO SUSAN

Contents

PREFACE   ix

1 WHAT IS AN OIL PROGRAM?   3

Explanation of terms. Why it's called an "oil program" and not a "drilling fund." Mutual funds vs. oil programs.

2 HISTORY OF OIL PROGRAMS   11

From $2 million in 1953 to $500 million today. Background period in oil development. The first oil program is organized. John M. King and the marketing period. The current maturing period.

3 STYLES OF PROGRAM MANAGEMENT   18

The two approaches: independent oil company and the oil investment manager.

4 TYPES OF PROGRAMS   28

Exploratory. Development. Balanced. Income programs.

5 MARKETING STYLE AND THE MARKET   40

Sales by officers and directors. Internal sales organizations. In-house programs. Brokers and dealers.

6 PROGRAM STRUCTURE AND OPERATION   51

Legal structure. Liquidity. Conflict of interest. Minimums and suitability. Assessments.

7 COSTS AND COMPENSATION   65

Sales and overhead costs. Incentive compensation. Front end interests. Overriding royalty. Net profits interests. Disproportionate cost sharing. Functional allocation. Disproportionate risk taking. Percentage of surrender value.

8 PERFORMANCE REPORTING   80

The shortcomings of the present system. Statistics. Cash flow. Present value analysis. The SEC position. The Oil Investment Institute approach.

CONTENTS
Continued

9 TAXES AND INVESTMENT ANALYSIS 91

The tax advantages of intangible drilling costs. Depletion. Capital gains. After tax cost. Investment analysis.

10 REGULATION OF OIL PROGRAMS 103

The Securities and Exchange Commission. Blue Sky agencies. National Association of Securities Dealers. Oil Investment Institute. Future federal legislation.

APPENDIX A 113

Members of the Oil Investment Institute

APPENDIX B 115

Statement of Business Standards and Compliance Guidelines of the Oil Investment Institute

APPENDIX C 128

North American Security Administrators' Guidelines for Registration of Oil and Gas Offerings

APPENDIX D 136

Fee structure analysis

APPENDIX E 151

How a typical program works

Preface

THE oil program industry has grown substantially since 1966. Since then it has raised more than $1-billion and become a major element in the search for oil and gas in the United States. For that reason, oil programs are attracting a growing interest from investors, brokers and oil people.

Unfortunately there has been no single source of information to which they can refer. There have been articles in trade journals, law reviews and elsewhere, but those articles tend either to be too technical or too shallow to be useful for the majority of readers.

I have attempted to write a book for people who know something about oil programs and who want to know more. While the information is not detailed, it should give the reader a good general understanding of how oil programs work. I have not focused on any particular aspect of the industry, but have tried to give a general overview of its inner workings.

I have tried to make an objective presentation of the oil program business, but my own opinions may occasionally color the discussion. I am Executive Vice President of Petro-Search, Inc. Petro-Search is an oil program management company with a particular point of view. It is an oil investment manager (see Chapter III) that has a balanced exploration approach (see Chapter IV). It is basically an "in-house" program (see Chapter V) that uses a limited partnership form with no surrender value (see Chapter VI). If my own company's approach is overly stressed, and I hope that it is not, at least fair warning has been given.

There are several areas, however, in which I refuse to be shy about my opinions.

First, I believe that one type of oil program—the development program with a goal of low risk through drilling near existing production—does not have a reasonable chance of being profitable to investors.

Second, I think that current performance reporting practices in the oil program industry are useless.

Third, and most important, I believe that there are some practices in the oil program business which, by virtue of their conflict of interest potential, ought to be illegal.

If any reader disagrees with these views, he may find himself muttering in discontent over two or three chapters.

It is difficult to know how to thank all of the people who have been helpful to me in the preparation of this book. There have been so many individuals involved in various stages that I can mention only some of them.

At Petro-Search, Dr. Ben Sutton, Ron Verlander, and Elliott Husney all provided useful comments and guidance. At Financial Service Corporation, Bill McMurry was very helpful—especially in the early chapters.

Miss Judy Learned is particularly deserving of my gratitude for the hours that she spent in transposing my illegible notes to typewritten form.

Mr. Don Taylor, General Counsel of the Oil Investment Institute, and Mr. Art Berner, General Counsel of Inexco Oil Company, also made suggestions which I hope led to a strengthening of the book.

Thad Thomas, author of *The Exploration Drilling Program,* was invaluable. His very thorough and thoughtful comments made an important impact in several areas.

Those who know my father will see how greatly his opinions have influenced mine. He has been active in oil program management since 1953, and I doubt that there is anyone in the industry who is more qualified to run an oil program than is Truman Anderson, Sr. To him I owe a large part of my knowledge of oil programs as well as my rather stern views on the relationship between investor and manager.

TRUMAN E. ANDERSON, JR.
January, 1972

OIL PROGRAM INVESTMENTS

1

What is an
oil program?

OIL program investing is now the most attractive tax shelter available to high income individuals and corporations. Its growth in recent years has been substantial. By the mid-1970's, it promises to be a $1 billion-a-year industry that will have an important effect upon the petroleum supply in the United States.

Yet, oil programs are a relatively new investment vehicle. They are not very well understood even by the investment community. They are viewed with considerable suspicion in the oil business. Certainly, the practices of a few program management companies have raised questions. The programs constitute a young and still unregulated industry, one which is in some ways similar to the mutual fund industry in the middle 1930's.

What is an oil program? The first obstacle to an understanding is the name. "Oil program," "oil and gas program," "oil fund," "oil and gas fund," "drilling program," and "drilling fund" have all been used. Each refers to the same concept.

In this and subsequent chapters, the term "oil program" will be used. The word "program" is preferable to the word "fund" because "fund" implies an inaccurate analogy to mutual funds. The word "drilling" is inappropriate because not all oil companies engage in drilling activities. "Oil program" is less accurate than "oil and gas program," but it is briefer.

An oil program is a diversified, professionally managed business that allows investors to benefit from the investment and tax savings opportunities available in the oil industry. The following are its principal characteristics:

1. It is a joint venture or limited partnership interest in a closed-end entity.

2. That entity explores for, develops, or buys properties which can produce petroleum.

3. The investment is a pro rata share with all other investors in the assets, profits, and losses of the program.

4. The organizational structure allows investors to participate directly in the profits and losses of the program.

5. The program is a pooling of a large number of investors' funds under professional management.

6. Tax savings associated with drilling operations are a major factor in the profitability of oil program investments (except for those programs which primarily purchase productive properties rather than drill for production).

7. Oil programs (except those which primarily purchase productive properties) are a suitable investment only for those in the higher income tax brackets.

Whether a joint venture or a limited partnership, an oil program is an operating business of a particular size. After the formation date of the program, participating interests are no longer sold. Unlike most mutual funds, an oil program offering is not open ended. That is, it does not involve a continuous offering of participating interests in the same entity. It is true that many program managers have continuous offerings, but those offerings are for a series of separate programs which are formed periodically.

This means that each program is a distinct organization. Although each does not have its own operating staff (these are provided either directly or indirectly by the program management company), the programs are in the oil business and function in many ways like an independent oil company. Some explore for oil. Others develop property with oil-bearing potential. A few simply buy already drilled wells. In each case, they engage in activities normally associated with active participation in the oil business.

An oil program investment is a pro rata share of the entity with other investors. It is a direct participation in the program. Consequently, it is an equity type of interest. If the program is highly successful, program investors will be the principal beneficiaries. If it is a total failure, program investors will have last claim on any remaining assets of the program. In this respect, a program interest bears a strong resemblance to common stock in a corporation.

4

The organizational structure of all oil programs must allow the direct flow-through of profits and losses to investors. If such a structure is not created, investors cannot participate directly in the tax advantages afforded to the oil and gas industry. This is just the opposite of the corporate form. A corporation retains its profits and losses and pays income taxes accordingly. An oil program does not pay income taxes; its investors include their pro rata share of profits or losses in their own income tax returns. The obvious purpose of this approach is to allow investors to have the tax incentives that accompany exploration and development of petroleum reserves. If an oil program were simply a corporation in the oil business, the nature and breadth of the market for program interests would be severely changed.

An important feature of oil programs is that they are under the control of professional management companies. Investors, therefore, have the benefit of the skills and experience of people who are presumably knowledgeable in oil investments. The investor probably has a greater chance of success in an oil program than he does if he tries to invest directly in drilling prospects.

A related and highly important characteristic of oil programs is that they provide diversification. Each program is the sum of relatively small investments by hundreds or thousands of investors. With funds far in excess of what a single individual could control, the program manager can give investors a share in a large number of prospects. Because of the frequency of dry holes in oil exploration and development, breadth of exposure is an extremely important advantage. Diversification in drilling prospects is even more important than is diversification between investments in securities.

Although not all forms of oil programs are tax oriented, most provide an important tax shelter for investors. Any program which expends a significant portion of its funds on drilling activities (as opposed to the purchase of producing wells) will generate substantial "losses" in the first several years. Those losses are deductible against taxable income and can be extremely valuable to investors in high income tax brackets.

This feature of oil program investing rests primarily upon the treatment of intangible drilling costs. Instead of being capitalized and written off over the life of any productive properties discovered with the program's money, many of the costs associated with the drilling of wells can be immediately expensed.

5

The availability of tax savings to oil program investors has the effect of defining the market for oil programs. In general, oil programs are a suitable investment only for those in the higher income tax brackets. An investor in the 50% tax bracket will profit considerably more than an investor in the 25% tax bracket in the same program. The program manager finds just as much oil for both investors, but he can save more taxes for the high tax bracket investor.

It should be mentioned, on the other hand, that tax savings are not a major factor in the programs that purchase producing properties. The tax advantages associated with drilling are not available to such programs. They must make money for investors without reference to these tax savings. Because they are able to do so, they appeal to a much broader market than do drilling programs.

Perhaps a comparison with mutual funds will make this description more clear. For many years, the oil program industry has made the mistake of referring to itself as the "oil fund" business. Since most people understand mutual funds, the analogy makes explanation easier. There are certain similarities between mutual funds and oil programs. The most important are:

1. Pooling of funds under professional management;
2. Broad diversification;
3. Direct flow-through to investors of profits and losses;
4. Pro rata sharing of profits and losses.

After that, the similarity stops. Taken further, the analogy becomes more a cause of confusion than an addition to understanding. Indeed, in 1969, Congress (at the urging of the Securities and Exchange Commission) considered subjecting oil programs to regulation under the Investment Company Act of 1940. That law was originally designed to regulate mutual funds. This move was based, in part, on the belief that oil programs are merely a specialized mutual fund. It was only with considerable urging from the industry that Congress and the Securities and Exchange Commission changed their position.

There is little question about the need for some kind of legislation to cover the oil program industry, but the use of a law aimed at mutual funds certainly was inappropriate. Some of the reasoning is expressed in this explanation:

"Notwithstanding the similarities, the differences between exploration funds and mutual funds are more apparent. . . . .Moreover, investments are in mineral properties, not securities, and involve mineral operations rather than the passive holding of a portfolio of securities. Mutual funds have their primary appeal to relatively unknowledgeable, small investors; whereas investors in an exploration fund are likely to be — and should be — relatively sophisticated and affluent. Exploration fund "managers" have nearly unlimited discretion in the selection of properties while the manager of a mutual fund is subject to some limitations under the Investment Company Act, and under the fund's policy as to the type of securities to be acquired. Finally, the exploration fund is typically a much more speculative investment than a mutual fund, largely tax motivated, and has substantially different objectives."[1]

This description is a good one, but it needs elaboration. First, the distinction between "mineral operations" and "passive holding of a portfolio of securities" is critical. An oil program management company actually runs a series of businesses in behalf of investors. It plays a much more active role in that respect than does the management of a mutual fund which invests in businesses, but does not attempt to run them. This fact alone means that oil program managers are faced with very different kinds of responsibilities than are mutual fund managers.

Second, it is obvious but important to point out that mutual funds are in the securities business while oil programs are in the oil business. Each industry has its own peculiarities. Each requires of its participants different knowledge and skills. Both need to be run by rules appropriate to their situations.

Third, oil programs are considered more speculative than mutual funds. This very common opinion, given one condition, is false. If only high tax bracket investors purchase oil program interests (and they are the only ones who should), then oil programs are not so speculative as they appear. This point requires explanation.

There are different kinds of risk. For example, the chance that a perfectly good investment could not be sold is a liquidity risk. The possibility that the management of a company might be incompetent or unethical is a management risk. The possibility that an investment in one well will be worthless if the well is dry is an investment risk.

The rate of failure in oil exploration and development is a widely known fact. Only about one out of every nine "wildcats" finds pe-

[1]Bloomenthal, Harold S., *Mineral Exploration Funds,* Duke Law Journal, Volume 1968, No. 2, pp. 199-200. Copyright 1968 Duke Law Journal. Reprinted by permission of the copyright holder and author.

troleum. Even fewer make significant amounts of money. It is on the basis of this kind of odds that oil companies have argued for the tax incentives given them under the Internal Revenue Code. Development of adequate petroleum reserves is vital to the defense and economic strength of this country, and the government has good reason to provide tax incentives to the oil business. What is important, however, is that this country *does* have tax incentives for oil and gas. Those tax incentives reduce the investment risk that originally justified their creation.

With respect to oil programs, the treatment of intangible drilling costs is the most important of these investment incentives. If the investor is in a high tax bracket and if he invests in a program large enough to provide broad diversification, the investment risk is not a serious problem because of his tax savings.

This is not to say that oil program investing is a sure thing. Far from it. What is meant is that, given certain conditions, the investment risk in oil programs is not so important as other risk factors — principally liquidity and management.

The liquidity risk arises simply because the assets of a successful oil program are marketable only over a long period of time. The typical oil well produces for a period of about 10 years. Without the use of some kind of financial device, the investor in an oil program will get back his investment and profit, if there is any, only as the wells belonging to the program pay out. Consequently, any investor who wants to get his money out fast will have a problem.

Program managers have tried to solve this problem by the use of "cash surrender values" and by conversion of program interests into common stock (after most of the tax incentives have been used up). The cash surrender values probably will not provide a lasting solution, even though they have been popular in recent years. They only transfer the liquidity problem from the investor to the manager and can create a serious problem for any program manager who has a large number of redemptions. Conversion of program interests to common stock in a publicly held company will probably be the answer for most programs in the future. Even in this case, there is a minimum of 2 to 3 years before the conversion can take place. After that, there will be, in some instances, a thin market for the stock.

What this implies is that oil program investors must be aware that they are investing in a basically and fundamentally illiquid type of asset. Unless they are prepared to hold on to their investment over a period of years, they should not consider an oil program.

Management risk is, at this stage in the development of the oil program industry, a more serious problem. Oil programs are regulated by two federal securities laws (the Securities Act of 1933 and the Securities Exchange Act of 1934), the securities laws of the various states, and to some extent by the National Association of Securities Dealers. Even within that framework, however, a number of practices have arisen which harm the interests of the investor. They are primarily in the area of conflict of interest and self-dealing and will stop only when they become illegal under a new federal regulatory law.

What kinds of oil programs are there? Many. Each is the creature of individuals who created it and reflects their business style.

Although there is quite a lot of detail, the various program types can be categorized under several major questions. They are: How is the money raised? How is it managed? How is it invested? What are the mechanics? The following is a list of the major possibilities in each of these categories:

1. *How is the money raised?*
   a. By officers and directors
   b. By an internal sales organization
   c. By an affiliated sales force ("in-house" programs)
   d. By broker/dealers
   e. By combinations of (a) through (d)

2. *How is the money managed?*
   a. Independent oil company style
   b. Oil investment manager style

3. *How is the money invested?*
   a. Exploratory programs
   b. Development programs
   c. Balanced programs
   d. Income programs

4. *What are the mechanics?*
   a. Legal form (limited partnership or joint venture)
   b. Evaluations and liquidity
   c. Minimums
   d. Assessments

     e. Compensation and costs
     f. Conflict of interest

Each of these subjects will be discussed in later chapters. All of them are important for two reasons. First, they influence the behavior of the program manager. Second, they determine the characteristics of the security being offered and, therefore, the financial need that is fulfilled for the investor.

For example, a company which relies primarily upon broker/dealers for its sales will gear its product to the desires of that group. Such programs tend to have a lower minimum investment, no assessments, some form of surrender value, and an inclination toward development drilling.

An equally important question is the status of the program manager. If it is an independent oil company looking for outside funds, its problems will be quite different from a manager whose job is management of programs only, but who does not have on his staff the technical skills of the typical independent.

Obviously, the investment philosophy of the program manager is important. An income program is at the far end of the spectrum from a program that emphasizes exploration. Both play an important role in the industry, but serve different investment needs.

Finally, it is important to understand the implications of the mechanics of the program. For example, the joint venture form raises the possibility of additional unlimited liability for the investor while the limited partnership form imposes restrictive transferability conditions.

The lack of regulation of the industry and the broad variety of business practices impose upon the investor, the broker, and the analyst some extra responsibility when they consider oil program investing. In one sense, it is their present low level of understanding about the oil program investment that restricts it from achieving the very important role it ought to play in both the securities and the oil industries.

2

History of oil programs

THE oil program industry is no longer an infant, but it certainly has not yet reached maturity. Total sales increased by 10 times between 1965 and 1971, but that growth is more indicative of insignificance a few years ago than it is of enormity now.

It is not a new idea to get a number of investors together to participate jointly in oil exploration. Promoters have been doing this since the first commercial oil well in the United States was drilled in 1859. It is only the manner in which such ventures are now organized and marketed that is new. Oil programs are an old product in a new package.

The following historical grouping is arbitrary, but it does reflect some meaningful patterns in the development of oil programs:

1) Prior to 1950 (Background Period)
2) 1950 to 1966 (Organization Period)
3) 1966 to 1970 (Marketing Period)
4) 1970 to present (Maturing Period)

Prior to 1950 (Background Period)

The 90-year period prior to 1950 saw enormous changes in the oil business. It started from a role as a competitor to whale oil for lamp fuel. It became a major international industry.

It is inappropriate here to attempt a detailed discussion of that period. However, a few observations can be made about the role of the passive investor in the years prior to the effective date of the first oil program in 1950. Hopefully, those observations can shed light on

11

some of the issues that still face oil program investors and managers.

Passive direct participation took a variety of forms. It might have involved common stock, royalty interests, some form of working interest, a net profits interest, a partnership interest or some other form of "participation." No matter what the format, two key features were constant: a "promoter" and a "deal" involving a limited geographic area with a relatively small number of wells. This approach is the clear predecessor to the independent oil company approach today. Many independents still sell privately to investors.

Some of these early ventures were highly successful. The chance of discovering a major field in the United States was substantially better 50 years ago than it is today. The occasional spectacular result made it easier for promoters to raise money. For a long time, tax savings were not a major factor.

This form of investment was, to a considerable extent, a boom or bust arrangement. Lack of diversification made potential results highly variable. At the same time, crude oil prices could fluctuate wildly. A new discovery could glut the market and drive prices down.

At times, oil investments took on the appearance of the California Gold Rush. Greed could easily take precedence over reason. The following account of the boom fever in Canada is a typical, if extreme, example:

"For months the newspapers had been full of conflicting reports as to whether or not a commercial discovery had been made. Stockbrokers' offices displayed samples of the oil to convince Calgarians that it really did exist. Several cars had used it for fuel, and actually ran. 'Experts' had been freely predicting that 'Calgary will soon be in the throes of one of the greatest oil excitements ever known.' Hundreds of thousands of acres of oil leases had been filed with the federal government, and the value of these leases was skyrocketing. There were riots in the Dominion Land Office as eager speculators lined up to file on anything available—even the municipal Bowness Park. Dozens of new oil companies had been formed, hopefully to drill on those leases, and shares were sold in the hundreds of thousands to Calgarians thirsting to get in on the ground floor and eager to part with their savings.

". . . 'many Calgarians are suffering from a mild form of insanity,' said the *News Telegram* in October, while *The Albertan* concluded simply that 'the city is oil mad.'

"But the excitement was nothing compared with what happened after

12

word reached Calgary on the night of Thursday, May 14, 1914 that this time the Dingman well had hit it for certain: oil.

" 'If the city was oil crazy on Friday,' said *The Albertan,* 'on Saturday it was demented.' *The Herald* noted that the stock promoters had 'struck a financial gusher,' which made the discovery well 'look like a lawn sprinkler.'

"All day and all night the crowds fought and struggled for precedence in the offices of the most prominent oil companies, and clamored for shares and yet more shares. Relays of policemen barely kept a clear passageway and there was never a moment when the would-be purchasers were not lined up three deep in front of the counters, buying, buying, buying."[1]

The discovery subsequently turned out less than a marginal economic success.

By the 1940's, the conditions had shifted entirely. Most of the "easy" discoveries had been made. As each year passed, the necessity for strong scientific work became more important. And so did federal income taxes. Excess profits taxes and the 91% tax bracket stimulated corporations and individuals to invest substantial sums in oil ventures. The tax shelter available in oil investing had been around for years, but not until the high tax trends of the 1940's was it used by investors in significant volume.

A new group of promoters and a new group of investors came into being. Typically, the promoter came from Oklahoma or Texas. He sought investors in the high income tax brackets. Quite often he sold marginal prospects at high prices.

The attitude of investors during that period was unusual. Since taxes were close to confiscatory in the high brackets, it made little difference to those investors whether the oil venture was successful or not. If it failed, the investor was not much worse off than if he had just paid his taxes.

By the early 1950's, investor attitudes began to change. The poor performance of many promoters increased the cynicism of some substantial investors. The cause was easy to discern: lack of professional management and inadequate diversification. The need for a better investment method was apparent.

[1] Gray, Earle, *The Great Canadian Oil Patch,* Maclean-Hunter Limited, 1970, pp. 55-56.

1950-1965 (Organization Period)

The first oil program became effective with the Securities and Exchange Commission in 1950. Blackwood and Nichols Company and Davidson, Hartz, Hyde and Dewey, Inc., in their prospectus of November 28, 1950, offered $3,500,000 in "Contributions in Oil Property Interests."

This first offering was obviously an oil program, but it certainly was unusual by current standards. No minimum investment was required. No provision was made for sales commissions. The prospectus contained no information on possible conflicts of interest, and almost nothing was said about the risks of oil program investments. Page 10 of the prospectus said, among other things, that:

"When oil property is acquired from the proceeds of contributions the same will be recorded in the names of the Contributors as joint owners thereof or in the name of one of the partners of the Partnership for the benefit of the Contributors. As such, the Contributors have the same liability with respect to such property as would apply to any other owner or owners of property."

Such an arrangement today would be unusual.

The Blackwood and Nichols program was an important step, because it was the first program registered with the Securities and Exchange Commission and available by public offering in several states. In structure, however, it was closer to a promoter's deal than a true oil program.

Although there are no records on the subject, it does not appear that marketing of oil programs was very successful during the 1950's. By 1956, only Apache, Austral and McCulloch were in the program business in a meaningful way. Oil programs had important advantages over the private deals of various independent operators, but very few people really understood what an oil program was. This was the most obvious deterrent to sales growth. It takes time for an idea to be accepted.

A second problem was that prospective investors were not accustomed to being sold a "fund." They wanted to look at specific prospects. The potential value of their investment in past deals was supposed to be determined by getting into detail on geology. A manager selling professional management and diversification aroused suspicion. This was compounded by the usual offering of

14

only joint ventures or general partnerships. Those organizational forms require a great deal more participation by investors than does the limited partnership. The limited partnership was not used until the 1960's because of a fear that it might be classified as an association taxable as a corporation by the Internal Revenue Service.

Oil programs had to be sold by officers, directors, or internal sales organizations. The brokerage community was not interested in selling oil programs—partly because of the lack of a "track record" and partly because they were not understood. Program managers were oil people with little experience in securities. This inexperience and the small number of people selling program interests doomed oil programs to insignificance for more than a decade.

1966 to 1969 (The Marketing Phase)

John M. King of Denver must be given credit for bringing oil programs into the open as an important factor in the oil and securities industries.

One observer of these developments, veteran Oklahoma independent oil operator William B. Cleary, gave the following account of what happened:

"Through 1967, the sales efforts of most funds were conducted by the offering company, although most had some provision for NASD broker sales with compensation to the selling brokers. Annual offerings prior to 1967 approached $50 million. In that year, the industry exploded.

"The man who lit the fuse of the bomb was John M. King of Denver, who had relatively limited success in prior years through his KS Funds offerings. King conceived the idea of a massive sales organization with participations in funds marketed along the same lines as mutual funds.

"Entrance fee was lowered so that small investors could be spread out over a number of months. Minimum participation was set a $1,300 initially with $50 to $150 paid per month.

"King took the position that a speculation in a drilling fund was not necessarily more risky than a flyer in a new stock issue—and there was no minimum limitation on such a stock purchase. The majority of sales were made through NASD dealers who received a 7.5 percent commission for those sales.

"Investor accounts were handled by a management company, which, in turn, contracted for the prospects the fund drilled. The management

15

company absorbed the sales fee.

"King's success brought a multitude of others into the business. Brokers realized a new source of commission income. Producers found a new and apparently simpler way to raise their substantial amounts of money."[2]

The following chart indicates what has happened since 1953 (note the increase between 1966 and 1967, the year that King began marketing by mass methods):

Estimated oil and gas program sales since 1953 are as follows:

1953	$ 2,000,000	1962	$ 22,000,000
1954	4,000,000	1963	30,000,000
1955	5,000,000	1964	40,000,000
1956	7,000,000	1965	35,000,000
1957	8,000,000	1966	45,000,000
1958	8,000,000	1967	115,000,000
1959	11,000,000	1968	340,000,000
1960	12,000,000	1969	500,000,000[3]
1961	16,000,000		

At the height of his sales efforts, King's two programs (Imperial American and Royal Resources) had dealer agreements (through an affiliate) with about 700 brokers. At the same time three competitors—Prudential Funds, Natural Resources and White Shield—raised tremendous amounts of money through networks of securities dealers. This success attracted more managers and more dealers to oil programs. There are now more than 125 program managers. It it doubtful, however, that more than one-third of that number will last in the business.

1969 to Present (Maturing Period)

There are several important reasons to believe that oil programs are nearing maturity.

[2]Cleary, William B., *The Oil Digest*, "Cleary Chief Traces History of Drilling Funds," Sept. 1970, p. 19.

[3]Anderson, Truman E., Sr., Hearings Before the SubCommittee on Commerce and Finance of the Committee on Interstate and Foreign Commerce, House of Representatives, 91st Congress, First Session on H.R. 11995, S 2224, H.R. 13754, and H.R. 14737, Serial No. 91-34.

The first is size. In late 1970, George Hardin, then president of Royal Resources, made some interesting comments in an interview with the *Oil and Gas Journal*. He said, in part,

"Although precise figures are not available, I think it is safe to say that at least 25,000 wells have resulted from the activity of funded drilling programs since 1966," Hardin said. This is a big hunk (8%) of the total 138,666 wells drilled during that time.

"There's no way to determine how much oil and gas have been found and developed by funded programs since 1966," Hardin said, "but even a pessimistic view . . . would lead to a conclusion of at least 500 million bbl. of oil or gas equivalent."[4]

Mr. Hardin's estimate is very inexact, but it does indicate the growing significance of oil programs to the domestic petroleum supply.

A second reason is the Oil Investment Institute (OII). Formed in 1969, the OII has taken affirmative and responsible action to upgrade the quality of oil programs. Its membership includes most of the larger programs. Those members subscribe to a "Guide to Business Standards" (see Appendix B) which provides an excellent set of ethical and business practices for the industry.

A third evidence of growing maturity is success of oil programs in attracting substantial oil and securities firms. In securities, such well-known organizations as Investors Diversified Services (IDS), Bache and Co., and Hornblower and Weeks, Hemphill Noyes, are aggressively involved. In the oil industry, companies such as Continental Oil (Conoco), Husky, Occidental, and Belco Petroleum have become actively engaged in program management.

There can be little doubt that oil programs are here to stay.

[4]*Oil and Gas Journal,* "Fund Companies May Rebound in 1971," November 2, 1970, p. 50.

3

Styles of program management

SEVERAL ways are available to provide the variety of services necessary to the investor in an oil program.

But first, what are these services? The following is a list of those that must be provided in one way or another:

    I. Financial
        a. Accounting and Tax
        b. Planning and Program Management
   II. Legal
        a. Securities and Exchange Commission
        b. Blue Sky Commissions
        c. Other Legal
  III. Sales and Public Relations
        a. Dealer Service
        b. Advertising and Promotion
        c. Direct Sales
  IV. Investor Service
        a. Reporting
        b. Administrative Services
   V. Technical
        a. Geology
        b. Land
        c. Drilling
        d. Operating
        e. Engineering

With the exception of planning and program management (Ib), a company can directly provide all or none of these services and still be a program manager. Those services it does not provide directly can be retained from other companies.

Certain of these services, in fact, are not ordinarily provided by oil program managers. As is the case in many industries, a good portion of accounting and legal work is done by outside firms. Most program managers rely heavily on outside help for Securities and Exchange Commission and Blue Sky work. In direct sales, program managers frequently rely on marketing organizations. Program managers are not normally geared for such an effort (although there are important exceptions). While investor service activities usually stay with the management company, the technical services peculiar to the oil business are often obtained from outsiders. For example, a fully staffed independent oil company may employ outside contractors to drill its wells. This is normal practice within the oil business and pertains as much to major oil companies as it does to oil program managers.

There is one important distinction between oil program management types that should be clearly understood. In the early stages of the industry, oil program managers provided all or most of the technical services. That is, geologists, land men and engineers were provided by the company itself. In the industry, companies organized in that manner are referred to as "independent oil companies" or "oil operators."

In 1960, the Prudential Fund organization adopted a different form. That company became known in the industry as an oil investment manager. This new type of organization allocated a portion of total funds raised to be spent with oil companies or "oil finders." The important difference created two distinct types: companies which provide technical services internally and those which rely upon outside companies for most of the technical services associated with the process of finding oil and gas reserves.

Both of these types of programs have played a significant role in the industry. On balance, the oil operator (independent oil company) approach has managed more dollars than the oil investment manager.

Independent Oil Companies

An example of the independent oil company which provides com-

19

plete oil and gas program services is INEXCO. The following from its Prospectus dated May 8, 1969, illustrates the point:

"International Nuclear (INEXCO), which will sell to the partnership substantially all the prospects, properties, and leases which the partnerships will explore and develop, has actively engaged in oil and gas exploration for one year, although the principals of International Nuclear have engaged in such exploration in prior years. International Nuclear currently has approximately 160 employees, 27 of whom are oil and gas geologists, 9 of whom are land men and 8 of whom are production engineers. The principal operating office of International Nuclear is at 308 Lincoln Tower Building, Denver, Colorado and branch offices are located in Oklahoma City, Oklahoma; Houston, Texas; Calgary, Alberta, Canada; and Casper, Wyoming."

Three major advantages are claimed for this type of approach to oil program management. They are:
1. Closer control;
2. Expertise of oil companies in their area of exploration and development; and
3. No middleman taking additional compensation.

The independent oil company supervises the day-to-day activities involving geological and other technical services. This gives it close control over the investor's dollar. Those providing these services for the investors are generally employees of the oil program manager, and thus there is direct accountability. Information also is readily accessible to the program managers. There is less necessity to rely upon the judgment and integrity of those outside of the direct control of the program manager.

In most instances, an independent oil company makes a decision to enter the program management business only after it is established as a company. It has already displayed its abilities within a certain geological area. An expert geologist in one part of the country, for example, might be a very poor geologist in another. It is important that the oil program manager have at his disposal people who are qualified to conduct operations in a particular area.

Generally, an independent oil company which has proven itself in a particular area is in a good position to provide investors with abilities backed by a good "track record." This has certain advantages both to the independent oil company and to investors. The larger amounts of money made available to the program manager means broader diversification for the oil company. At the same time, the merger of interests affords a broader diversification to investors.

An additional advantage claimed for independent oil companies over oil investment managers is the absence of any middleman. After overhead expenses have been covered, the principal method of compensation for the oil program manager in all cases is an economic interest in the oil and gas found for the investor. With the independent oil company approach, this happens once. Only the independent oil company obtains an economic interest in the reserves developed. The investor shares only with the program manager. But in the oil investment manager approach, the investor shares both with the manager and with the oil finder.

The principal disadvantages of the independent oil company approach are:

1. Limited diversification;
2. Greater potential for conflict of interest;
3. Inability to invest large amounts of money;
4. A tendency to use oil finders to a significant extent anyway.

Even under optimum conditions, the oil exploration business on a well-by-well basis is risky. The only way to ensure reasonable success is to acquire a broad exposure to a large number of prospects in a large number of geological areas. So, if an independent oil company has ability only within a particular geological area, the diversification afforded to an investor is restricted. On balance, independents do not have access internally to as much talent over as broad an area as does the oil investment manager.

A wholly different category of problems involving independent oil companies is posed by conflict of interest. Some independents who manage programs are also in the oil business for their own account. This represents two potential types of conflict.

Independent oil companies, in the first place, may be tempted to favor investment prospects which indirectly benefit the program manager. For example, an oil program management company might put its investors into an exploration area but maintain for itself a large acreage position in adjacent regions. In this manner, the independent oil company could have the oil programs prove the value of its own acreage without taking any risk.

The second potential type of conflict with an independent oil company is self-dealing. There can be substantial profit for the oil company whether the investors make money or not. When an independent oil company provides services to investors at market value (or perhaps at higher than market value) the program manager is in a position to profit considerably. For instance, some independents lease equipment to their programs. The price at which that equipment is leased may or may not be fair market value. If it is not, the investor presently has very little way to find out.

One problem in judging independent oil companies is this: they sometimes act more like an oil investment manager than they first appear. The King Resources oil programs were in this category. In the normal course of business, most oil companies will take a certain number of drilling prospects from other companies or individuals. Even a program manager who initiates what is considered to be a large portion of his prospects internally may rely upon outside companies for a third to a half of all his investments. If this happens, not only is the investor subject to the double compensation because there are at least two compensation charges on the drilling prospect, but also he must cover the overhead both of the initial promoter and of the independent. At least in the case of the oil investment manager, there is no double charging for exploratory overhead.

Another disadvantage of the independent oil company approach is natural limitation of the amount of money it can invest intelligently. The independent may not be able to build a competent staff at a rate proportionate to its growth in sales. Indeed, this has been and continues to be a serious problem in the oil program business. A company's success in selling large amounts of program interests does not mean the company has grown at a similar rate in its capacity to invest those funds intelligently. This problem, obviously, is more severe for the independent if it attempts to spend all of the money it raises internally.

Despite these disadvantages, approximately 80% of the top 25 oil programs in 1969 were of the independent oil company type. The explanation is simply that oil programs have become a popular way for independents to raise funds for their operations.

Oil Investment Managers

An example of the oil investment manager which relies on the services of oil finders is Hanover Planning Company, Inc. Its Prospectus of April 3, 1970 indicates its plan of operations:

"The company will not maintain a staff of geologists, landmen, petroleum engineers and other specialists such as is usually maintained by Third Party Operators. Consequently, the company will not originate prospects, but will acquire prospects originated and submitted by Third Party Operators. In order to assure the acquisition of prospects located throughout widespread geological areas, the company may enter into partnership agreements, sharing agreements, and joint ventures with a number of Third Party Operators, many of which will have had experience in specific geographical area. In selecting prospects, the company will utilize the staffs of such Third Party Operators and, in addition, may retain as independent consultants to the company, geologists, geophysicists, and petroleum engineers familiar with the particular areas involved."

The advantages claimed for the oil investment manager approach are the following:
1. Broad diversification;
2. Flexibility;
3. Ease in administration;
4. A strong emphasis on performance;
5. Capacity for the intelligent use of large amounts of money; and
6. Lack of conflict of interest.

With the same amount of money, the oil investment manager generally is able to provide a broader diversification than is the normal independent oil company. This is so simply because the investment manager works through a larger number of geologists in a larger number of areas. The investment manager gets an exposure in more geographic areas to more types of prospects. Since diversification is an extremely important element in any successful exploration program, this is a decided advantage. Of course, if the independent oil company is large and has effective offices in many places, this advantage of the oil investment manager is reduced.

Flexibility is another clear advantage of the oil investment manager approach. It's considerably easier not to renew contracts with oil finders than it is to open and close exploration offices. Also, if for one reason or another the management of an oil program decides to allocate its funds to a different area, it can do so with more ease than can an independent oil company. These companies simply can't leave staffs stranded in various parts of the country.

Ease of administration is a third significant advantage of the oil investment manager. The management type does not get bogged

23

down in day to day detail. True, the independent oil company has closer control. At the same time, the oil investment manager, by not getting involved to such an extent, has the opportunity and time to become a professional manager of oil investments and not a professional administrator of an oil company. The oil investment manager who learns to recognize a good oil finder in a good oil-finding area and who knows how to deal in those areas may well be ahead of the independent oil company managers who must be involved in the more detailed aspects of the oil and gas exploration business.

The oil investment management approach can aggressively emphasize performance. If a particular oil finder does not perform, there is no problem in breaking off business with him. This may not be done so easily with a staff geologist, engineer, landman or attorney. Over a period of time, the oil investment manager can compare the finding cost of oil for the various operators with whom it does business. Those finding costs yield an accurate evaluation of performance.

This advantage is not available to the independent oil company. The independent can close unproductive offices, but it takes longer. Acreage inventory must be disposed of, people sent to new jobs or fired, the personal aspect of which is a deterrent to rapid action. Just as a matter of practicality, it's harder for the independent to act rapidly in this kind of situation.

Perhaps the single most important advantage for the oil investment manager is lack of problems in the area of conflict of interest. The investment manager does not engage in the oil business for its own account. It does not do business either directly or through affiliates with its investors except as the manager of the investors' funds. It has a much more restricted area of instances where it can profit while its investors do not.

The oil investment manager, too, can more easily create an identity of interest with the investor. Compensation normally is geared to performance. The manager does not have other ways of making a profit from the investors' dollar. A properly drawn relationship between an oil investment manager and oil finders also will create an identity of interest between the manager and the oil finder. This implies that neither the oil program manager nor the oil finder can profit unless and until they perform for investors. In the independent oil company arrangement, there is opportunity for profit whether the investor profits or not.

24

Finally, it appears that independent oil companies must either become oil investment managers or in good conscience limit the size of their growth. Independent oil companies, by their nature, have only a certain investing capability. In some instances, this is not a real limitation because their capability is so much beyond their ability to sell program interests. In other cases, the independent is not able to develop enough prospects of the proper quality to expend the investments of the participants. In such an instance, the independent oil company either will do a poor job for its investors or will be forced to become an oil investment manager on a relatively inefficient basis.

Before discussing the disadvantages of the oil investment manager approach, it is appropriate to point out that the distinction between oil investment manager and independent oil company is not so clear as this discussion may indicate. Not all the advantages apply equally to all companies of a given category. Take Apache Corporation — which has to be classified as an independent. The company's Prospectus of January 7, 1970 reveals that:

"Apache currently employs 47 geologists, geophysicists, engineers and landmen plus additional clerical and support personnel in its exploration activities."

Yet, Apache does not engage in the oil business for its own account. Its technical staff develops prospects for the programs. Consequently, the company does not have the conflict of interest problems that afflict other independent oil companies.

Two major criticisms have been leveled against the oil investment manager as an approach to oil exploration program management. Thad Thomas, referring to this approach as the "mutual fund" type of program, mentions those objections:

"The writer prefers the "oil company" form of drilling program management above the "mutual fund" organization. Preference is based on the fact that "mutual fund" management purchases drilling prospects at a price that generates profits to the consultants, then management takes its own profit for services rendered . . . because of the double overhead aspect, this writer cannot recommend the "mutual fund" drilling program.
A second factor that limits the desirability of the "mutual fund" program relates to management functions. The chief duty of the manage-

ment of a "mutual fund" program is to select companies that will perform actual drilling and/or to evaluate drilling prospects submitted by outsiders. The management group does not actively generate drilling ideas. The "mutual fund" investor, therefore, has no real method to evaluate the skills of the prospect-generation group. He can only evaluate how well management has picked successful oil finders in the past."[1]

Of the two objections, the more serious is obviously that the oil investment manager interposes a middleman. In the usual case, the oil investment manager will take an overriding royalty from all of the production developed for the investors. In addition, the oil finder will retain an economic interest, usually in the form of a carried interest, in any reserves developed by that oil finder. The investor must absorb the cost of the overriding royalty to the manager and the carried interest to the oil finder.

It should be pointed out that overhead is not a factor. The oil investment manager usually will pay the overhead cost to the oil finder. The independent oil company has that overhead internally. Although some evidence indicates overhead incurred in developing drilling prospects is less for the oil investment manager than it is for the independent oil company, not enough data is available to make a strong claim.

It's simply an unarguable fact that there is more than one level of incentive compensation in the oil investment manager approach. The question is whether advantages of the oil investment management approach outweigh this problem. Because oil investment managers are good partners and negotiate from a position of strength, total compensation paid to the oil program manager and the oil finder may not differ greatly from the compensation paid to the independent oil company. Failing that, it's an open question whether the broader diversification, increased flexibility, ease of administration, performance orientation, capacity for large investments and lack of conflict of interest outweigh any additional costs.

In the end, of course, only the performance of these two types of programs will prove their merits. But it is quite evident that the oil investment management approach has more of a role to play in the industry than some independent oil companies believe. Oil program

[1] Thad W. Thomas, *The Exploration Drilling Program,* The Tax Shelter Newsletter, pages 147-148, 1969.

management is a natural evolution for independent oil companies. This does not imply that only oil program managers that evolve from independent oil companies are proper managers.

Thad Thomas also suggests that oil investment managers really are not directly responsible for the performance of their programs because they must rely upon the skills of their oil finders. It is not clear why this is a problem. From the investor's point of view, if performance is the same, it doesn't matter whether he is hiring people who are skilled at finding and negotiating with oil finders or whether he is dealing directly with oil finders. The different approach may be of some interest to the investor in his analysis of a program, but there is not necessarily a great virtue in having a geologist run an oil program.

Summary

Both the independent oil company and the oil investment manager are capable of doing an excellent job for their investors. Each has certain inherent advantages and disadvantages of which all investors should be aware.

The future growth of both the oil program business and the independent oil industry in this country will be influenced by the extent to which one or the other of these types of programs grow more predominant. At the present time, independent oil companies hold a larger share of the oil program market. Whether that will continue depends upon the performance of these two program management styles and their sophistication in reaching the oil program market.

4

Types of
programs

THE most important decision facing the oil program manager concerns his investment policy. Once that decision is made, his program can be categorized. From that point on, he has defined his market and identified certain possible advantages and disadvantages of his approach.

The investment policy decision rests principally on two factors: (1) risk taking and (2) the attitude toward immediate income.

Four types of oil program can be defined:
1. Exploratory
2. Development
3. Balanced
4. Income

Exploratory Programs

An exploratory program is one whose major activity is the search for new petroleum reserves.

That search is generally in areas that are untested. Consequently, the typical exploratory program will probably drill more dry holes than productive wells. The income from those few productive wells, however, may far exceed the cost of the dry holes. With high risk of failure comes high potential gain.

The exploratory program is the least likely to develop an immediate cash flow. This is so for two reasons.

First, it may be looking for oil and gas in areas which do not have a readily available market. The Prudhoe Bay discovery in northern Alaska is an excellent example. Certainly the initial discovery well at Prudhoe Bay was an exploratory (wildcat) well. Present indications are that the first barrel of oil will not be sold from that well until 5 or 6 years after the well was completed. Obviously, immediate cash flow was not a motivating factor for the group that discovered this enormous field. Just as clearly, however, the long term benefits will be extremely great.

The second deterrent to immediate cash flow is that the discovery must be developed. A discovery well is only the beginning in a long process of tapping the new reservoir. That process involves an expenditure of large amounts of money in the drilling of subsequent wells. The natural source for those funds is the cash flow developed by the initial wells.

In general then, the exploratory program is one which is prepared to take high risk prospects with a possibility of a large return and which is willing to defer income in order to develop fully the reserves that the program may discover.

Perhaps the clearest statement in a prospectus of the investment policy of an exploratory program is that of Royal Resources Exploration, Inc. in its Prospectus of May 12, 1970. The Prospectus says:

"It is expected that the capital of each limited partnership will be used principally to acquire and explore oil and gas properties that are not part of a known commercial reservoir or deposit in an effort to locate, develop and exploit new reserves of oil and gas.
In the event of a completion of an exploratory well as a producer, it may be desirable or it may be required by the terms of the lease (leases usually carry such a requirement) to drill one or more development wells offsetting the initial well. If the limited partnership has sufficient capital to drill such a development well or wells, it may use partnership capital for that purpose. However, if sufficient capital is not available for drilling of development wells or if, in the judgment of the management company, it is in the best interest of the partnership to do so, the limited partnership may for such purposes utilize its own net cash receipts, borrow monies from banks and other lending institutions, grant farmouts to others, enter into agreements for dry hole and acreage contributions, or conduct drilling operations jointly with other independent and major oil companies. It may be necessary or profitable, in some instances, for a limited partnership to sell a lease on which a discovery well has been drilled and leave development operations to others . . . . ."

The nationwide success ratio on exploratory wells is about one in nine. One in 40 proves to be an economic success. These facts have implications for the market for exploratory programs and for the manner in which programs ought to be organized.

A purely exploratory program is best suited to investors in very high income tax brackets. Such programs run a relatively higher risk of failure. Therefore, their investors should be those most able to afford a loss and those that will lose the least. An investor in the 70% tax bracket who invests $10,000 can reduce tax liability by as much as $7,000. An investor in the 40% tax bracket with the same investment would save $4,000 in taxes. In the event of a total failure in a program, the 70% bracket investor would lose $3,000 while the 40% bracket investor would lose $6,000.

Because exploratory programs are best suited to high tax bracket investors, it is particularly important that a method be provided to take any profit as a capital gain rather than as ordinary income. If an exploratory program finds and develops large reserves, additional ordinary income would be least desirable from the investor's point of view. He would be much better off, for example, if he were able to exchange the program interest for common stock in a publicly held corporation. He could then sell his stock at a gain whenever he wishes.

A properly managed exploratory program has an excellent chance of doing well for investors if broad enough exposure is available. If the chances of a commercial discovery are one in 40, then the investor needs an exposure to far more than 40 exploratory tests. This implies that the program manager should take a small interest in a large number of prospects rather than a large interest in a few prospects.

The investor should avoid putting all his money in one exploratory program. If a program manager has a series of partnerships or joint ventures, the investor should invest in several of them rather than in just one. In addition, he should stay away from programs which raise a small amount of money. A program that has $1 million can get a much better exposure than one that has raised only $250,000.

Exploratory program investors should be prepared to wait for income. If a discovery is made, additional funds may be necessary for development of the surrounding acreage. Since it is unlikely that income from the initial wells will be adequate, production loans may also be necessary. This will delay the initial income distributions. In fact, a successful exploratory program may need additional funds from investors. Although assessable program units are not popular, they are certainly justified in the case of exploratory programs.

Development Programs

A development program is one whose principal activity is the development of existing petroleum reserves rather than the search for new reserves.

Such programs are inclined to drill in areas about which there is a lot of geological information available. There is normally production in the area, and the odds of having a successful well are substantially higher than in an exploratory program. On average, semi-proven and proven prospects are successful 50% to 75% of the time. This advantage may be offset by the fact that the cost of entry into proven and semi-proven areas is higher. The value paid for leases and any carried working interest, net profit interest or royalty interest may be a function of the production or lack of production in the area.

Development programs generally take smaller acreage prospects since large acreage prospects are not available. A typical development prospect, for example, would be a 40-acre offset to existing production. In such an instance, there would be no doubt about the existence of petroleum in the area. Success or failure would hinge upon whether or not the initial reservoir can be tapped at a location not too far away from existing productive wells.

A significant advantage of development programs is their capability of creating cash flow quite rapidly. There already is a market in the area by the time that a development program becomes interested, so access to a pipeline is not a problem. Furthermore, development programs are more inclined to drill small acreage prospects that provide little or no opportunity for additional development. This means that there will be no claim upon the cash flow created by successful wells for continued development of the reservoir.

In general then, a development program is one which attempts to get production from proven or semi-proven areas. In so doing, it is able to generate cash flow at an earlier time than exploratory programs, but is less able to provide an opportunity for a high return on investment.

31

Equity Resources of Los Angeles makes the following typical statement in its Prospectus of June 22, 1970:

"At least 90% of the properties to be acquired and drilled will be on semi-proven and proven acreage. Not more than 10% of the properties will be on exploratory leases or acreage involving exploratory or 'rank wildcat' wells. . .

"Although both prospective and producing properties may be included in the program, the partnership may not invest more than one-half of its contributed capital in properties which are producing oil and gas in commercial quantities at the time of acquisition. At present, the General Partner has no specific intent with respect to the amount of partnership capital, if any, which may be invested in producing properties within the foregoing limitation (see Article IV). No producing properties were acquired by any of the prior programs."

This description is typical of oil programs which are oriented toward development drilling. Some programs will buy a considerable number of productive properties along with drilling of development wells.

The growth of development programs accounts for a significant portion of the oil program industry's growth since 1965. In 1969, development programs provided approximately $260 million of the industry's total sales of $500 million. In 1970, development programs probably accounted for 40% of the industry's sales. All five of the top five money raisers in 1969 (Clinton, Prudential, Imperial American, White Shield, and Natural Resources) were development oriented.

There are several explanations for this success. The most important is that development programs are the easiest way to provide what really interests most program investors—the tax write-off. They can also incorporate such favorable features as early evaluations, lack of assessability, high early write-offs, and a high level of apparent safety.

Development programs are an appropriate investment primarily for those who are interested in tax savings. Most such programs provide a poor chance of significant profitability beyond the tax savings.

From the investor's point of view, the ideal development program is one which maximizes write-off and provides early cash surrender values. The investor could then continuously take his tax savings, redeem, and reinvest for additional tax savings. The principal problem with this approach is that, if enough investors follow it, either the program manager will have to change his redemption feature or he may be driven out of business by demands for cash in excess of what he can provide. This subject will be discussed in more detail later.

Balanced Programs

A balanced program is one which drills both exploratory and development prospects.

It diversifies the types of drilling prospects that it takes by risk category. On the one hand, it attempts to create some underlying value for investors by drilling in relatively low risk, low reward areas. At the same time, it shoots for bigger reserves with another portion of its budget. In the first few years, such a program will develop a level of cash flow probably higher than a typical exploratory program, but lower than the typical development program.

Balanced programs are managed with the intent of taking advantage of the opportunities afforded by exploratory and development programs. Whether or not they benefit from the favorable aspect of exploratory and development drilling or are caught in the disadvantages of both of these approaches depends upon the skill and the luck of the management.

The Hanover Planning Company Prospectus of January 22, 1971 states the investment approach of the typical balanced program:

"Purpose of the 1971 Hanover Drilling Fund, Series 5, Agreement.
"In the initial phase of the Program the Company expects the operations conducted by it under the Agreement to be exploratory in nature. The Company will acquire on behalf of the Participants Prospects originated and submitted by Third Party Operators (who will conduct all drilling and other operations thereon) and will enter into agreements with Third Party Operators covering the operation of producing Leasehold Interests and other property interests. The Company estimates that between 40% and 45% of the proceeds available for use in the Program will be utilized in the financing of the drilling and completing of exploratory wells and a like amount of such proceeds will be utilized in the financing of the drilling and completing of development wells. The Company expects a large number of such development wells to be drilled on Prospects where the drilling of exploratory wells thereon under the Agreement resulted in the discovery of oil and/or gas in commercial quantities.

If at some point in its conduct of the Program the Company determines that the exploratory wells theretofore drilled have not resulted in the discovery of production in commercial quantities sufficient to afford the participant a return on the aggregate Subscription Price paid by the Participant, the Company will look for and acquire for the Program low risk Prospects which the Company in its best judgment would expect to afford the Participant with such a return."

In contrast to exploratory programs, balanced programs are more likely (1) to drill their own development wells on discovery acreage, and (2) to take development drilling prospects.

The exact policy varies from program to program. However, a total balanced program regards degree of risk as another element which requires diversification. The manager will take drilling prospects from a broad range of risk categories.

Ideally, what the balanced program manager can do is acquire sizeable acreage positions in exploratory areas. With some portion of his total budget he can then test the acreage. If his initial tests are successful, he will generate for the programs lower risk prospects (since they are close to the initial discoveries) on relatively inexpensive acreage. If the initial exploratory phase is a failure, the unallocated portion of the budget can be used to drill development prospects in other areas. This activity is not as profitable, but it can assure that the program will not be a total failure. Petro-Search Exploration & Development Program, Series A, states such an objective as follows:

"In the oil business, the Petro-Search approach is something called 'elephant hunting'. Petro-Search will, on occasion, seek major finds (with the attendant risks) in participation with other companies.
What Petro-Search tries to do is to underpin the investor's net cost (an arbitrary figure which reflects the investor's net dollar exposure after allowance for his tax savings). This underpinning is achieved through investment in lower risk, lower reward, semi-proven and proven type prospects. After that, Petro-Search goes 'elephant hunting'."

This type of approach makes it possible for investors in as low as the 40% tax bracket to invest in balanced programs. On the upside, a balanced program could do as well as a successful exploratory program if its success is obtained early. On the downside, the investor will probably lose (in a well-managed program) no more than the amount that he has exposed after allowance is made for tax savings.

34

Although risk of total loss is lower in a balanced program than in an exploratory program, investors in both should have basically the same objectives and expectations. Diversification between programs is important. Certainly, the investor should be prepared to hold his program interest for at least several years. Neither should he expect any income distributions for a few years. Indeed, he should be quite pleased if the program manager needs to assess him for development of program discoveries.

Income Programs

The income program is a different category of oil program. It does little drilling and primarily buys producing properties. It lacks the tax advantages of drilling oriented programs and appeals to a different market. At the same time, it is obviously the most secure in predictability of results.

Such programs are created not so much because of their low risk (although that is an important feature), but because of their potential for creating income. Income programs are created for the purpose of developing partially tax sheltered income for investors. Although organizationally and functionally they are quite similar to oil drilling programs, they are, in an important sense, a different kind of investment vehicle.

Oil and gas income programs are a new development in the oil program industry. Many programs have the option to buy existing production as part of their total investment portfolio. Very few have concentrated exclusively upon purchase of productive properties. One of the first such programs to be filed with the Securities and Exchange Commission was Petro-Lewis Oil Income Program. Its Prospectus of July 28, 1970 indicated that,

"The General Partner intends that the Partnerships will acquire producing oil and gas properties in the United States and in Canada. The initial emphasis will be in the Rocky Mountain region. Purchases may be made elsewhere if desirable opportunities appear. The Partnerships will not engage in exploratory or development drilling.
"The Partnerships may purchase any kind of interest in the producing property. In most cases, the interest acquired will consist of all or part of the rights and obligations under oil and gas lease. Occasionally, a Partnership may purchase royalty, overriding royalty and other non-operating interests. The Partnerships may also purchase interests in

35

partnerships or entities holding producing properties, including entities sponsored by the General Partner or an affiliate."

Although income programs do provide some writeoffs (principally by having a deductible management fee), they are not intended to be a tax shelter. As their name implies, their purpose is to give investors an income oriented security.

Since the cost of proven, productive properties is high, cost depletion rather than statutory depletion is normally used. There is no more tax advantage to cost depletion than there is to straight line depreciation. It simply reflects the fact that the petroleum reservoirs decline in value as petroleum is produced.

Particularly in times of high money costs, income programs can be attractive to investors. In effect, a production purchase is a purchase of an estimated declining income stream over an estimated period of time. The purchase value of that income stream is a function of the cost of money (discount rate) and the earning power required. An important limitation is that engineering evaluations of the future income stream cannot be wholly accurate.

Because the income from oil and gas wells declines at an exponential rate, income to investors will also decline. The typical oil well in the United States lasts about 10 years; the typical gas well may last for 15 years. After that period, the well is shut down and no more income is available. During that period, the amount of income will decrease from year to year.

Income program investors must be aware that proceeds available to the program include both return of capital and return of income. They will not recover their initial investment in one lump sum at the expiration of the program. Each program investor will receive some of his original investment back as part of the program's cash flow.

For example, distributions amounting to 25% in the first year do not necessarily imply a 25% return. The rate of return must be determined after deducting depletion and depreciation from operating income. This is so because the depletion and depreciation approximate the amount of original investment being returned (assuming that cost depletion and straight line depreciation are used).

Identifying Program Types

There are two problems in identifying program types.

The first is the tendency among program managers to define their terms differently. Because of the high risk character of a pure exploratory program, an exploratory program manager might call a well "exploratory" when another program might call it a "field extension" or a "step-out." The reason is that the exploratory program manager may want some level of security. On the other hand, a development program might drill what would normally be called exploratory prospects just to have a shot at higher stakes.

The second problem is that the differences between exploratory, balanced, and development programs are matters of degree and not of kind. As a matter of policy, some oil program managers invest 70% of their funds in exploratory prospects; others will invest 60%; others 50%; some 10%. At some point, an arbitrary decision has to be made whether the program still can be regarded as exploratory. A series of programs managed by the same manager may be more or less exploratory, balanced or development. In many instances, the character of a program will depend upon the quality and type of drilling prospect that becomes available when the program has investable funds. With the same investment philosophy from program to program, the same program manager will have different kinds of prospects in different programs.

In a study of 101 oil programs by Resources Programs Institute the following breakdown was made:

Oil Programs Classified by Investment Policy[1]

Exploration Dominant	41
Development Drilling Dominant	17
Producing Property Purchase Dominant	1
Secondary Recovery Dominant	1
Balanced: Exploration & Development	30
Balanced: Exploration & Development & Property Purchase	11
TOTAL	101

This study indicates that balanced programs are the most common type of program. (It should be noted that some programs where exploration is dominant are still balanced programs.) However, the information is misleading in one sense. Although only 17 of the 101 programs had a dominant development drilling policy, those 17

[1]Resources Programs Institute, *Compendium of Oil Drilling Programs,* March 1970.

37

programs represented some of the larger programs in the business.

Why Have Development Programs Taken the Largest Share of the Market?

No firm figures are currently available on industry sales either from the Securities and Exchange Commission or from the Oil Investment Institute. Nevertheless, an informal study of industry sales indicates that development programs (including those who invest a significant portion of their funds in producing properties) accounted for 58% of the market in 1969. In 1970, they accounted for something less than 50%.

Certainly development programs merit investor attention, but this success appears disproportionate to the advantages such programs have to offer.

The typical development program offers little chance of significant profit. Its principal virtue is that it provides tax savings to investors with a minimum risk of serious loss (if the program is properly managed). For that reason, it should appeal to those investors more interested in tax savings than in capital appreciation. Simply because of the economics of development in the United States, it is unlikely that a development program manager can consistently return one dollar of present value per dollar invested. This makes it particularly important that development programs have relatively low overhead and compensation charges. Too high a cost to investors in either of these categories makes it almost impossible for the development program manager to deliver reasonable results.

The success of development programs is probably the single clearest instance of the effect of marketability upon program managers. The sales successes in recent years can be attributed, in large part, to the increased effort of the broker/dealer community. In return for their support, program managers have been under pressure to make their product as marketable as possible.

Probably the single most important asset that development programs have had in the marketplace is that they reduce investor anxiety. Most investors know very little about the oil business, but they do know that drilling for oil is a chancy affair. Most development programs can show a record of more successful wells than dry holes. To the extent that investors are concerned primarily with the tax write-off (and most of them are), they see development programs as a safe way of achieving their objective.

A second incentive for buying development programs is that they can provide accurate evaluation of program interests earlier. Exploratory and balanced programs, because they operate in new areas, cannot provide reliable data to investors for several years. In the meantime, the investor in a development program does have a clear idea of the value of his program interest. No matter what his investment philosophy, the program manager who can tell investors what they have is in a better position to sell his product.

A third reason for this success is that development programs are able to begin payment back to the investors sooner. There is no great need for additional development, and development programs are not normally assessable. This certainly is desirable from the investor's point of view.

For the oil program manager, a development program is the easiest to administer. He is principally a "deal taker." His prospects are over small acreage. It is simply a matter of taking a prospect, drilling it and either putting it on production or plugging and abandoning it. In contrast, an exploratory or balanced program will take much larger acreage positions where a single well will not necessarily test all of the acreage. In short, exploratory and balanced programs operate more like major oil companies.

Unfortunately, oil programs that are designed from a sales standpoint are often inherently less capable of doing a good job for investors in the long run. It has been said, with some justification, that the real security in a development program is the security in knowing that the investor will not get all of his money back.

Even the "performance" section of oil program prospectuses furthers this impression of safety. The program manager is allowed to report his success ratio (the relationship of successful wells to total wells drilled), but he is not allowed to report how much oil and gas he has found in those wells. Unfortunately, it is in exactly that area that development programs tend to fall short. There is no particular virtue in drilling a series of successful but only marginally profitable wells.

Perhaps as the brokerage community and the investing public learn more about oil program investing, they will feel less inclined toward development programs.

Professionally managed exploratory and balanced programs have an acceptable level of investment risk, and they provide investors with a much better opportunity to make a significant profit.

5

Marketing
style and
the market

THE change in marketing style since 1965 has been the principal contributor to oil program sales growth. Prior to that time, few brokers or mutual fund distributors actually sold oil program interests. That group now accounts for a large portion of total sales.

Five different marketing approaches can be identified:
1. Sales by officers and directors
2. Internal sales organizations
3. "In-house" programs
4. Broker/dealers
5. Combinations of one through four

None of these methods is inherently superior to any other. However, each does have some effect upon the structure of the program and upon the behavior of the oil program manager.

It is important to recognize from the start that these marketing styles are not mutually exclusive. For example, a company might well get substantial sales from officers and directors, from an internal sales force and from brokers. Strictly interpreted, there are probably very few oil programs whose approach does not fit under number five (combinations of one through four). Nevertheless, most oil program marketing is dominated by one of the four approaches. It is quite rare to find programs whose source of sales is not primarily from one distinct group.

Sales by Officers and Directors

In the early stages of the oil program industry, officers and directors were the principal fund raisers. Oil program investing was a novel concept, and the leaders of the industry had to do some selling before others would get involved.

The experience of Apache Corporation (Apache Corporation was one of the first companies to sell oil program units publicly) is instructive. In its first few years of operation, Apache's sales were made almost exclusively by officers and directors. The internal sales force that developed from that approach is now only a part of Apache's total sales effort. Since then it has gone into the broker/dealer community for additional marketing.

Of the many programs registered with the Securities and Exchange Commission, some still are sold primarily by officers and directors of the offering corporation. According to J. Lawrence Muir, Chief of the Oil and Gas Section of the Securities and Exchange Commission, "in 1969, 14 (9.6%) of the programs undertook the sale of their securities themselves; 49 (33.8%) used underwriters; 83 (56.8%) used their own staff plus unnamed members of the NASD."[1]

Major, Giebel & Forster is an example of a program sold by officers and directors. The program's Prospectus of March 19, 1970 states:

"The subscription for limited partnerships participation will be solicited by the General Partner of the partnerships. If subscriptions are accepted from selected members of the National Association of Securities Dealers, Inc., the commissions paid to such dealers will not constitute a reduction of the funds available for the purpose of the partnership, but will be paid to such NASD members by the General Partner out of its 5% management fee. There are no plans to actively solicit subscriptions through NASD members and there have been no arrangements or underwriting agreements with any securities dealer. Consequently, the amount of commissions to be paid to any such NASD member is not ascertainable."

Major, Giebel & Forster is an independent operator. For a number of years prior to its first publicly offered oil program, it had individual investors who participated in annual drilling ventures. Consequently, this program really involves organizational change in the treatment

[1] The Tax Shelter Newsletter, "Public Oil and Gas Drilling Programs." Notes of an address by J. Lawrence Muir, Securities and Exchange Commission, April, 1970.

41

of participants by an independent oil company. The program managers simply determined that an oil program approach is easier to administer than was the privately offered joint venture used in earlier years. The company has a built-in market for its program units from prior years and is not primarily interested in developing a broader sales base.

Programs marketed by officers and directors are normally smaller and less diversified than the average oil program. The program manager is experienced in a particular geological area, but probably does not drill in as many areas as the larger program.

These comments have an important exception. Clinton Oil Company of Wichita, Kansas, has raised substantial sums of money ($100 million in 1969). It is more than just an independent operator trying to supplement its annual exploration budget, yet a large portion of the funds raised by this program was generated by officers and directors.

Selling by officers and directors is probably the easiest marketing style to administer. It normally involves a few people who report directly to the management company. It keeps the sales force closely in touch with management and ensures that sales people are familiar with the program.

On the negative side, marketing through officers and directors restricts the amount of sales an oil program manager can expect to get. Although it is the easiest way to sell, it is limited in what it can do.

Internal Sales Organizations

There are two kinds of internal sales organizations. A few are retailers; most are primarily wholesalers. In both cases, the organizational format involves a subsidiary company; that is, a member of the National Association of Securities Dealers (NASD).

At the present time, only Apache Corporation develops significant sales from an internal retail sales organization. This approach can be interpreted as an extension of sales by officers and directors. It has most of the advantages and disadvantages of that approach.

Usually, an NASD member subsidiary is a wholesaling entity used by program managers who are distributing through a broadly based broker/dealer market. An example of such an arrangement is the Aaron Corporation, a subsidiary of Natural Resources Corporation. The Natural Resources Fund, Inc. Prospectus of August 20, 1969 reports:

"Aaron Corporation, a Colorado Corporation with offices at 500 Denver Club Building, Denver, Colorado will act as distributor for the Plans. All of its outstanding shares are held by the fund. The Plans will be sold through brokers and securities dealers who are members of the National Association of Securities Dealers, Inc. The distributor will charge a commission of 7½% on each sale, retaining for its own account a one-half of 1% commission and paying the remaining 7% to the dealer making such sale. In addition, Aaron will pay the dealer on account of Plans sold by such dealer and still in effect, an annual plan maintenance fee in an amount equal to the sum of ⅛ of 1% of the cash liquidating values of partnership interests acquired under such Plans at the end of each full calendar quarter during each year."

Recent experience in the oil program industry indicates that a strong wholesaling organization is a prerequisite to substantial marketing success. In most instances, program managers have found it impossible to raise more than $1 to $2 million per year without wholesaling support.

"In-house" Programs

An increasingly popular marketing method is the so-called "in-house program."

A typical example is the Occidental Petroleum — Putnam Fund relationship. Their Prospectus of August 7, 1970 explains that these two companies have entered into a partnership to offer oil and gas exploratory programs. The Putnam Oil Company (which is associated with the Putnam group of mutual funds) is the principal distributor of the program interests. Occidental Petroleum is the program manager. The two companies share any profits generated through management fees earned by the oil program.

Actually, two types of such programs can be identified. On the one hand, there are program management companies which are owned or controlled by a marketing organization. Equity Resources, for example, was a subsidiary of Equity Funding, a major mutual fund distributing organization. On the other hand, such large companies as Investors Diversified Services and Westamerica Securities have agreed with oil companies to market a program. The oil pro-

43

gram manager is independent of the sales organization, but the program manager and the sales organization share in the fees of the program either through a partnership, joint ownership of a corporation, or some other arrangement.

An in-house program creates an identity of interest between the marketing organization and the program manager. With such a relationship the marketing organization usually sells only one program.

There is a corollary for the program manager. In a sense, he becomes exclusive as well. Other marketing companies may not be willing to sell for a program so closely involved with a competitor.

From the program manager's point of view, this approach has several distinct advantages. First, it gives him a relatively broad exposure through a larger sales force than he could develop himself. Second, because of the close relationship with the marketing organization, the quality and continuity of sales tends to be high, and the program manager can exercise control over the training of the sales force. In addition, if the sales force is large enough, it may provide him with enough sales to fit his needs. However, if the marketing group is not large enough, the arrangement may well prove to be a liability because it will restrict him in marketing through other organizations.

Brokers

The most substantial growth of oil program sales in recent years has been sales by brokers. The term "brokers" is used in a broad sense to include brokerage houses, mutual fund distributing organizations, and other companies oriented toward the sale of securities. In short, it includes any group not directly a part of the oil program management company that is involved in the sale of securities.

In recent years, some of the most successful money raisers in the industry, including Imperial American, White Shield, Prudential and Natural Resources, have marketed their interests through a network of brokers.

This marketing style bears one very important similarity to "in-house" programs; it uses the same kind of organizations — usually large brokerage or mutual fund companies. The difference is that there is no exclusive relationship between the program manager and the distributor. That advantage is overcome by obtaining a large number of distributors who are served by a large wholesaling force. The two King Resources oil programs, for example, are reputed to have had over 700 dealer agreements at the height of their sales effort.

This marketing method has the greatest potential. Although it is not easy to penetrate the general brokerage market, if that penetration is achieved, the rewards can be substantial.

At the same time, some important limitations to this marketing style exist. They are:

1. The program manager cannot control the sales force and the manner in which his product is sold;
2. The sales force is usually the least well-trained;
3. Sales are the least predictable and the most unreliable, because of the loose ties between the program manager and the distributor.

This last problem is a particularly dangerous one. Even the very best of oil program managers can have a bad program or a bad year. If his sales are reliant upon the performance oriented brokerage market, his bad years may generate marketing disasters.

The Effects of Marketing Upon a Program Manager's Behavior

There are important differences between the program manager's "ideal" program and the one which a sales organization regards as best. This disparity arises for quite understandable reasons. The program manager wants an easily administered, profitable program. The sales organization wants a program that is easy to sell and has a broad market. Those objectives are not always compatible.

The result is a compromise on a number of program features. Normally, the program manager structures his program as he sees fit, but he must pay careful attention to the needs of those who sell his program. For that reason, some moves are made by the program manager primarily to increase the marketability of his product. For example, it is administratively easier and less costly to have one program a year rather than four or five. Yet, many oil program managers do have multiple closings annually — primarily because they need to provide continuous merchandise to sales representatives. It is much more difficult to keep sales organizations' interest and attention when there is just one closing a year.

Similarly, the sales organizations often exert the most influence in assuring that the program manager's compensation is competitive. Compensation is a complicated subject which dealers are more likely to understand than are investors.

Another instance of program structuring to meet marketing needs is the frequent omission of assessments. Most exploratory and balanced program managers would agree that assessments are the best way to finance development of exploratory successes. Yet assessments do not make oil program interests easier to sell.

These and other features of oil programs need to be considered in the light of what dealers and investors want. On such issues, none of the alternatives is inherently superior to the others. It is more a matter of balancing of interests. The program manager wants to maximize his sales by making his product as marketable as possible. On the other hand, neither responsible dealers nor investors want to impose restrictions upon the program manager which make it impossible for him to operate.

Unfortunately, the issues mentioned are the easy ones. They represent the legitimate interests of the various individuals involved in an oil program. As such, it is fair to claim that there is a bargaining relationship between the program manager and the dealer who must represent both his own interests and the interests of his clients.

The plain fact is that most investors, without professional advice, are not in a position to evaluate an oil program. This is so for two reasons. First, it is a new and complicated investment. Second, information is not available on a clear, consistent basis that is in any way meaningful to investors who do not have first-hand knowledge of the oil business.

This implies that generally it is up to the dealer (and, of course, to state and federal regulatory agencies) to see that the investor is not unfairly treated. In at least two instances, however, there is not an identity of interest between the investor and the sales representative. In such cases, there is a possibility that the investor's interests will not be regarded. They are: (1) instances in which the marketing organization has some economic interest in the management company and (2) instances in which the dealer is more concerned with the maximizing of his short term sales than with the long run interests of his investors.

This first situation is the more obvious, but in practice, it has been the less dangerous. In the last several years, this arrangement has become increasingly popular. In many instances, highly respected brokerage firms or mutual fund distribution organizations have acquired an interest in an oil program. In general, their associated programs have treated investors in a manner comparable to or better than programs not associated with a dealer. Indeed, it can be argued that such relationships are helpful to investors since such sales organizations tend to seek out and deal with the more responsible program management companies. Nevertheless, there is a certain tension between the investor and dealer interest which must be carefully watched.

Actually, the real problem is more subtle. It is a problem which all dealers face in some degree. For obvious reasons, a sales organization wants a security which is easy to sell to a broad market. Unfortunately, an oil program interest that fits these conditions is not necessarily in the best interest of the investor. This implies an odd fact about oil program sales: Investors tend to like certain features of programs which are not in their own interest.

No other single fact can more clearly indicate that the oil program industry is still in the educational phase of its growth. Unlike mutual funds where the question is "Which one?," oil program investors are still asking "What is it?"

In fact, the programs that seem to have met the least resistance in an uneducated market have the following characteristics:
1. Development oriented (high success ratio);
2. Low minimum investment;
3. Cash surrender value;
4. Early evaluation of program interests;
5. Generation of early cash flow;
6. High early write-off.

There is a strong argument against each of these features.

The problems of a development program were mentioned in an earlier chapter. What those problems amount to is that development programs have had too large a share of the market in the past. The success of an investment with such a low potential reward stems largely from the belief that it is safe because it results in few dry holes.

No issue has raised more questions with regulatory agencies than have those of minimum investments and investor suitability. As a tax shelter investment, oil programs (excluding income programs), are geared to high tax bracket investors. Clearly, that group includes a restricted market. Some dealers may want a program structure below a reasonable minimum standard in order to broaden the market.

One expression of finite requirements to cover this problem is included in the Guide to Business Standards of the Oil Investment Institute, an association of oil program companies. It reads as follows:

"Petroleum exploration and development programs involve risk of loss to public investors and are, therefore, ordinarily suitable only for those investors who are in a financial position to accept this risk.

"1. Interests in oil programs are ordinarily an appropriate form of investment only for persons with substantial other financial resources and annual income taxable in the higher income tax brackets. In general, therefore, interests in an oil program are deemed to be suitable for the investors to whom they are offered if, but only if:

"A) Each investor is required to make a minimum payment to the program of at least $5,000 (in one sum or in installments) during the first twelve (12) months of the program's existence.

"B) Each investor is required to supply written confirmation that:

1) He has a net worth of at least $200,000; or

2) Expects to have annual income of which some portion (not taking into account any deductions to be realized through participation in the program) is subject to income taxation at a federal rate of not less than 40% or an aggregate of city, state, and federal taxes of not less than 50%; and

3) That the investment is to be made solely for the personal account of the subscriber (or, in the case of a natural person, his spouse) and that the subscriber has no present agreement, understanding or arrangement to subdivide the interests subscribed for or to sell any portion of it to any other person.

"2. It is recognized that, even though the above criteria are met, an investment in an oil drilling program may not be suitable for a particular investor. Fulfilling the above requirements shall not dispense with, nor act as a substitute for, the independent duty of the person selling or recommending the purchase of a participation to determine that the recommendation is suitable for such investor on the basis of information furnished by such customer after reasonable inquiry concerning the customer's investment objectives, financial situation and needs and any other information known by such person selling the interest."

It is clear that oil program interests are not geared to a broad market. The manager and the dealer cannot ignore the suitability of a program investment for a particular investor.

Liquidity has always been a problem for oil program investors. The nature of the underlying assets of the successful program (petroleum reserves) can produce an income stream over a long period of time. In general, however, it is difficult to make an immediate sale on reasonable terms of the discounted present value of that income stream.

This fact has been a serious obstacle to oil program sales since it restricts the market to those who are reasonably sure that they won't need to "cash in" their investment.

In the last few years, the cash surrender value has been developed to minimize this problem. Either the program manager or subsequent programs provide the money to cover redemptions. In either case, there is a serious problem with any full-blown cash surrender value. If redeemed units are sold to subsequent programs (a practice prohibited to members of the Oil Investment Institute), there is a substantial conflict of interest problem as well as a possible reduction of the write-off available to subsequent investors. If the program manager buys the units, he simply assumes the liquidity risk himself. The problems in the last year or two of programs which assumed this burden display the potentially disastrous results. In those instances, the investors have most certainly been harmed.

For understandable reasons, brokers have found it easier to sell units with cash surrender values. This is so primarily because investors will shy away from an investment in which they are locked in. Unfortunately, the answer to the liquidity problem does not appear to be in the use of cash surrender values. The healthier answer seems to be that investors should not invest in oil programs if there is a reasonable possibility that they need to get their money out within several years. Many brokers would prefer that this not be the case.

Without going into detail, certain other problem areas can be mentioned. For example, dealers and investors prefer early evaluation of program units. For important technical reasons, however, accurate early evaluation (within 2 to 3 years) is not possible for exploratory and balanced programs. Therefore, the program manager must either guess or drill in proven areas. Guesses can be misleading, and drilling in proven areas reduces profit potential for investors. Similarly, there may be a pressure to create an early cash flow for investors. There are many instances in which early cash flow is not the best measure of profitability. An early return of cash might be achieved only at the expense of giving up long term value.

Finally, and quite obviously, there is an incentive for the program manager to maximize write-off. This particularly is the case for those brokers and investors who buy primarily to save taxes. Since the easiest way to maximize write-off is to drill dry holes, the program manager must obviously balance the need to create value with the need to save taxes. If the incentive to save taxes becomes a predominant decision-making principle, the program manager will make very bad economic decisions.

6

Program structure and operation

IN order to understand the functioning of oil programs, certain subjects relating to structure and operation need to be mentioned. Although the following list is not complete, it does include the more important issues that are not discussed in other chapters.

1. Legal structure
2. Liquidity
3. Conflict of interest
4. Minimums and suitability
5. Assessments

Legal Structure

The important element of providing tax shelter to investors carries definite implications as to how an oil program must be organized. It also introduces some legal traps which program managers must avoid.

All major oil companies are organized as corporations, yet not a single oil program is so organized. The reason for this difference is clear: The program must be organized in such a manner that the tax advantages (principally the treatment of intangible drilling costs) can be passed on pro rata to investors rather than retained within the entity.

This broad requirement can be met in several ways: Sub-chapter S corporations, general partnerships, mining partnerships, limited partnerships and joint ventures can all be used. In practice, only two organizational forms are employed. They are the limited partnership and the joint venture. This was reaffirmed by Resources Programs Institute which found the following in its study:

Form of Vehicle[1]

Limited Partnership	63
Joint Venture	36
Two-Tiered (limited partnership/joint venture)	2
	101

The principal characteristics of a joint venture are:
1. The interest is a pro rata share of the assets of the venture rather than a pro rata share of the entity that owns the assets.
2. Participation in management is either by active or passive consent.
3. The investors can be liable for obligations beyond their initial contribution.

The principal characteristics of a limited partnership are:
1. The interest is a pro rata share of the entity that owns the assets rather than a pro rata share of those assets.
2. The limited partners have no control of the management of the partnership.
3. The investor is not liable for any obligations of the partnership beyond his initial contribution (plus any income for his interest retained by the partnership).

There is much more to be said about the two organizational forms, but most of it is legal and technical beyond what needs to be covered here.

Limited partnerships have two distinct advantages over joint ventures: ease of administration and limitation of investor liability.

Neither the investor nor the program manager should want the investor to participate in program management, but a joint venture requires some effort in that direction. At the very best, the program manager must communicate in great detail with investors. Generally, he must request the investor's assent to the drilling of every well. That request takes the form of a description of the prospect, its cost, and any other information that seems necessary. Unless the participant indicates that he does not want to participate, he joins in the drilling of the well and owns a portion of it.

This procedure is an administrative burden to the program man-

[1]Stewart, Frazier M., Resources Programs Institute, *Oil Digest,* July 1970, page 18.

ager. It is costly and reduces his flexibility. In the final analysis, investors should rely upon the judgment of the program manager. Most investors do not have the ability to make such decisions. That is one of the reasons why they invested in the first place. This is not the only administrative problem, but it is undoubtedly the most serious.

The liability problem, however, is the more dangerous. As Thad Thomas points out:

"The legal distinctions between the two forms are very subtle and difficult to distinguish. In general, however, it is good practice—from the investor's point of view—to avoid joint venture drilling programs. Limited partners risk only the amounts they invest. Therefore, the limited partnership is, generally, a much safer investment vehicle. Drilling program management functions as the General Partner and agrees to indemnify all losses above and beyond what the investor contributes. The joint venture investor—on the other hand—is, generally, liable for his share of losses in excess of the amount he invests . . . including the cost of a drilling catastrophe, such as a blow-out which causes a major fire, pollutes a city's water supply or destroys a public beach after an oil spill. The joint venture is usually insured, but insurance coverage, if inadequate, may place the investor's personal fortune in peril."[1]

Although the joint venture seems clearly to be inferior, it still accounts for an important portion of the total oil program industry. There are two reasons for this. First, oil men are accustomed to joint ventures. Independents who enter the program business have used joint venture agreements with other operators in the past. Limited partnerships, on the other hand, are new to them. Very few standard oil transactions outside the program business are structured with a limited partnership. Second, limited partnerships have become usable only since about 1960. For a long time, there was a severe tax problem. A question persisted whether the Internal Revenue Service would classify oil program limited partnerships as associations taxable as corporations. This classification would be ruinous because it prevents the flow-through of tax losses to investors. Joint ventures have never had so severe a problem in this respect. It has only been in the last few years that most limited partnerships have been some-

[1]Thad W. Thomas, *The Investor's Guide to Oil and Gas Drilling Programs;* 1970, page 14.

what safer from adverse rulings.

The desirability of a limited partnership comes from the fact that it approaches the corporate form without being taxable as a corporation (because profits and losses flow through to investors). However, the program manager must be very careful to structure the partnership to avoid having the Internal Revenue Service classify it as an association taxable as a corporation.

In the last several years, the IRS has become more stringent in its requirements. In order to get a favorable ruling, the partnership must show that it conforms to standards designated by the IRS. It must show that the limited partners do not own too much of the general partner in order to avoid making the general partner a "dummy." Conversely, the general partner should not own too much of the limited partnership interests. If it does, the general partner and the limited partners run the risk of being basically the same entity. The general partner, because of its unlimited liability, must have substantial assets. Creditors of the limited partnership must have access to a reasonable asset value if their demands are unpaid.

It is particularly in this last area, substance of the general partner, that has been a source of trouble for the industry.

The joint venture must also avoid being classified as a corporation, but this has not been as much of a problem for joint ventures as it has been for limited partnerships.

Liquidity

The growth of oil programs since 1965 has been accompanied by increasing attempts to solve the liquidity problem inherent in oil operations. Unlike a mutual fund investor who can redeem almost immediately, the oil program investor is faced with limitations imposed by organizational form and by the nature of the asset he holds.

Until recently, oil programs were necessarily regarded as long term investments. The initial investment was recovered through oil run income. Oil run income is income earned as oil and gas are produced and sold. Since the average well lasts 10 to 20 years, quite obviously, the return of total investment is a lengthy process.

Since joint venture or limited partnership interests are not easily marketable, the investor could not expect to sell his investment unless the program manager was willing to buy it. If he was willing to do so at all, it was not on favorable terms to the investor and was subject to availability of capital on his part.

In recent years, two important methods of increasing liquidity have gained popularity. They are the so-called cash surrender value and the exchange for common stock.

A typical cash surrender value is described in the Natural Resources Fund Prospectus of August 20, 1969:

"Cash Liquidating Value. The "Cash Liquidating Value" of a Planholder's interest in each limited partnership, shall be his proportionate share in each partnership determined as the sum of:

(a) Cash on hand, plus

(b) Prepaid expenses and accounts receivable (less a reasonable reserve for doubtful accounts), plus

(c) Market value of proven developed reserves of oil, gas and other minerals, royalties, overriding royalties and other producing interests in oil, gas and mineral properties (determined as set forth below), plus

(d) The lower of (i) 80% of the net book value of all other assets, or (ii) market value thereof less cost of sale, as determined by an independent appraiser (determined separately for each asset), MINUS

(e) An amount equal to all debts and obligations of every kind and nature including accrued expense and other liabilities of the partnership (which shall be deducted from the total of (a) through (d) ... As of the end of each calendar quarter the Fund will have a licensed professional petroleum engineer (who may be employed by the Fund or Leben) estimate future net revenues from properties described in (c) above held by each partnership and determine the present worth of such future net revenues using a 6% per year interest factor, provided that the interest factor may be increased or decreased by the same percentage as any increase or decrease in Federal Reserve Bank Discount Rate established by the Board of Governors of the Federal Reserve System subsequent to June 30, 1968. For the purposes of this paragraph the market value of such limited partnership properties at the end of each quarter shall be 70% of such present worth of the estimated future net revenues."

The advantages to the investor are obvious. This redemption feature substantially lessens the liquidity problem. At the same time, it has created a tendency on the part of some investors to liquidate their investments as soon as redemption values are published. They look at the investments as strictly a tax shelter and continually redeem and reinvest. Since this practice increases the commission to brokers, there are strong incentives for redemption.

These redemptions create an important problem. Unlike mutual funds, it is not normally practical to cover redemptions by liquidating assets of the program. The program manager himself must come up with the money. That money must either come from the company itself or from new sales. To the extent that redemptions are covered out of new sales, the program manager is introducing a whole new set of problems.

The program manager can get cash from two sources: internally or through subsequent sales. If redemptions are not great, or if the manager has large amounts of cash available for this purpose, he can make use of the cash surrender value. If not, the success of the surrender feature will breed its own destruction.

In the past, some important programs have used new sales as a source to cover redemptions. However, those new sales are in new programs. A new program is a separate operating entity and what it does, in effect, is to invest its funds in older programs when it buys out redemptions. This approach has two major disadvantages. First, it reduces the write-off available to the purchasing program (thereby penalizing its investors). Second, it creates an incentive for the program manager to publish surrender values that may be above the true worth of the program interests. Since the program manager does not buy the interest and since good surrender values are exceedingly valuable in producing sales, a clear conflict of interest arises. It is for this reason that the Oil Investment Institute, the trade association of oil and gas programs, has taken the position that sales to subsequent partnerships of redeemed program units are unacceptable business practice.

There is a final danger in surrender values that needs to be considered. In many respects, surrender procedure can be regarded as a feature put into programs to facilitate marketing. To the extent that programs depend upon a broad based marketing network, the more likely they are to have a surrender feature. The general brokerage marketing approach is also the most "fickle." It probably involves the least educated salesmen and clients.

The results can be disastrous. The problems of John M. King's Imperial American Fund in 1970 are instructive. Severe cash shortages on the part of King Resources and the involvement of Mr. King with Investors Overseas Services developed a severe drop of confidence in Imperial American. The result was a very large request for redemptions which only multiplied the liquidity crisis within the King complex of companies.

In the long run, the exchange of program interests for common stock, not the surrender value, probably will provide a lasting solution to the liquidity problem. In recent years, such companies as Prudential and McCulloch have used this method with satisfactory results.

An exchange for common stock is simply an exchange of program interests from one legal form to another. After the exchange, the program is no longer a joint venture or a limited partnership, but a corporation. Since most of the tax advantages of an oil program are used up in their first 2 or 3 years, a corporate form is not dangerous to investors' interests after that time. Of course, since common stock is a very easily traded form of interest, it can significantly help in the liquidity problem.

An important limitation to the conversion of program interests is that it generally cannot be used for 2 to 3 years. The corporate form does not allow the flow through of tax savings to investors. Since it takes 2 to 3 years to use up most of the advantages of the treatment of intangibles, an exchange prior to that time would curtail the tax shelter effect of oil program investing. Even after that time, it involves a loss to the investor due to the effects of depletion (although, theoretically, the value of his stock would be enhanced to the extent that depletion would make the corporation in which he is a stockholder more profitable).

The exchange for common stock, however, provides a healthier answer to liquidity. This is so because it creates a redemption (sale of the stock in the open market) which is paid for by other investors rather than by the program manager or subsequent programs.

If this method becomes more popular, it creates an intriguing prospect. If industry sales in the 1970's settle between $500 million and $1 billion per year and if most of that is ultimately converted to corporate form, how many oil companies of large proportions will be spawned by this seemingly small part of the oil industry today?

Conflict of Interest and Self-Dealing

In the last several years, much of the criticism of oil program managers has centered on conflict of interest and self-dealing. The

57

practices have been discussed in Congress and studied by the Securities and Exchange Commission. They were in large part the motivating factor for creating a Guide to Business Standards by the Oil Investment Institute.

Despite disclosure requirements under the Securities Act of 1933, oil programs have not bared their souls to the extent that they should. This is so because the S-1 Form (Registration Statement) which must be filed by every publicly offered oil program does not ask the right questions. The Securities and Exchange Commission has recognized this and has begun work on a new form to make the required disclosure more meaningful.

To a large extent, the potential for conflict of interest is inherent in the oil program business. This is particularly the case for independent oil companies who manage programs. While it is acting as an agent for the investor, a program manager or its affiliates may be directly involved for its own account in the oil business and may be selling services to the program. This kind of relationship is subject to abuse. Unfortunately, some programs have acted inappropriately.

Several examples should make this clear.

A typical independent oil company will have exploration and development activities in addition to those it supervises for the program. This raises a variety of conflict of interest problems. Consider the following two:

1. The geological staff will generate prospects which need to be tested by drilling. The same staff is responsible for providing prospects both for the program and for the company itself. Which ones go to the program and which to the company for its own account? If a prospect of extremely high quality is developed, should it be drilled for the benefit of company stockholders or for the benefit of program investors?

2. Large expenditures can be justified in the oil business simply for the information that they acquire. A dry hole can be an extremely valuable investment if it provides geological information that points the way to later discoveries. This creates an interesting temptation for program managers. Why not purchase lands adjacent to acreage that is being drilled upon for the program? If the program's well is productive, the manager has an offset. If it is dry, the geological merit of the manager's land has been downgraded at no cost. This approach is a simple but effective way of letting investors take the risk of proving the value of the manager's acreage.

Self-dealing is a special form of conflict of interest. The following are two instances:

1. Every oil program must rely upon outside services. In some instances, the program manager or its affiliates may provide some of those services. For example, an affiliate of the program manager might be a drilling contractor. It is obvious that the contractor will drill wells for the program.

This makes the program manager both a buyer (as agent for the program) and a seller (as an affiliate of the drilling contractor). However, his own economic interest, at least in the short term, lies more with the seller than with the buyer.

The problem extends beyond the simple matter of how much is to be paid for the contractor's services. Might not the program manager decide to drill prospects of lesser geological merit simply because of their proximity to idle drilling rigs? Would he develop a field faster than is prudent to keep rigs running?

2. The industry practice known as "turnkeying" has to be regarded in some instances as self-dealing. A turnkey drilling arrangement is one in which one party agrees, for a fixed price, to deliver a well to the purchaser at a specified depth. If the well is not delivered as specified in the agreement, no money is due the party who undertook to turnkey the well.

This arrangement can be looked upon as a kind of insurance. In some areas, there are important technical and geological reasons that make it difficult to drill to the depth desired. Since there is risk, the cost of the turnkey arrangement will exceed the cost of drilling the well.

Some program managers turnkey wells for their investors. In so doing, the manager buys a service from himself with the investor's money. Obviously, there may be a temptation to charge the program at a rate above what the risk really entails. Or, it may induce a program manager to turnkey wells in low risk areas where prudent oil practice would normally rule out the use of turnkey arrangements.

It is important to emphasize that there is a strong distinction between potential and actual abuse of such a situation. There are reputable companies and program managers who have conflict of interest and self-dealing potential. It depends entirely upon the manner in which such relationships are treated.

The oil investment manager is in a better position to avoid such problems than is the independent oil company. The typical oil investment manager has no affiliates that are directly involved in the oil business. It is in the business of managing programs for investors and lacks the opportunities for abuse that face the independent. There is no other area (with the exception of performance reporting) that could be more easily straightened out by uniform and adequate disclosure. Unfortunately, this has not yet been achieved.

The Oil Investment Institute has taken the position that all charges for self-dealing transactions must be at cost or market. It has also held that, to the extent reasonably possible, the program manager must create an identity of interest with his investors. Although these standards do not go far enough, they certainly are a step in the right direction.

Minimums and Suitability

The tax incentives available to oil program investors make the investment appropriate primarily for those with substantial taxable income. The risks associated with petroleum exploration and development are significantly reduced by the tax shelter. Consequently, it has become customary in the industry for responsible program managers and sales representatives to recommend oil program investments only to those in the higher tax brackets.

It should be understood at the beginning that drilling and income programs must be distinguished. Since income programs are not tax oriented, they must stand on their own investment merit. They cannot rely upon tax savings to investors as a way of providing a return on investment. At the same time, a properly managed income program is relatively low risk. This means that income programs are suitable for a much broader market than are drilling programs.

The best way to assure that a program investor qualifies is for the sales representative to know his customer. Every case is different, and the appropriateness of an oil program investment is dependent upon the circumstances.

Despite the fact that responsibility for the qualifications of the investor must lie with the selling agent, some oil programs have created mechanical means of helping to assure investor suitability. These means are minimums and suitability tests (examples of such rules are given in Chapter 5).

The purpose of a minimum investment is to make oil program investing too expensive for all except the wealthy. The typical minimum investment is $5,000. Many small investors cannot afford an investment of this size and are automatically excluded. Despite the fact that minimums are far from perfect in weeding out unqualified investors, they can do a fairly effective job if set at a reasonable level.

In the last several years, some of the larger programs have had minimums in the range of $1,000 to $2,000. This level is clearly inadequate to screen out unqualified investors. In those cases, the desire for a broad market apparently was more influential than an interest in performing for investors. Although a significant minimum may be healthy from the investor's point of view, it does not necessarily contribute to the profits of brokers or program managers.

If it were possible to have a perfectly drafted, perfectly enforced suitability requirement, a minimum investment would be unnecessary. The normal procedure is a suitability test to determine the investor's income tax bracket and net worth. The purpose of such a test is to go directly to the issue of investor qualification. The investor's tax liability and net worth are reasonable indications.

Minimums and suitability guidelines can be useful, but they have important limitations. Consider the following example: XYZ Program

1. has a $5,000 minimum,
2. requires a 50% tax bracket or,
3. a $200,000 net worth.

Suppose that a young bachelor wants to invest in the program. He has taxable income of $22,000 in the 50% bracket. Because he is unmarried, he reaches the higher tax brackets more rapidly. With a minimum investment of $5,000 he is forced to the imprudent step of investing 23% of his income in one place. His married counterpart, on the other hand, has to commit only 11% of his income.

Although the tax bracket test is the single best one, it also has deficiencies. The first is practical. At the time the investment must be made, the investor may not know his tax bracket. He knows his earnings in the prior year, but he can only guess at what will happen in the current one. This is a more serious problem than it might appear for three reasons. First, a large part of the oil program market is suitable only by virtue of a few thousand dollars of income. Second, the best time to invest in a program is early in the year (giving the manager as much time as possible to maximize write-offs)

61

when income is least predictable. Third, the single biggest investing group is the medical profession — and many doctors have income that varies from year to year.

A second problem with tax bracket requirements is that they tend to look only at federal income tax rates. They frequently ignore the fact that state and city tax rates may be relevant. An investor in a state with high income tax rates is more likely to need an oil program investment than an investor in a state with low (or non-existent) income tax rates.

Serious questions can be raised concerning the usefulness of net worth requirements in measuring suitability. The intention is to ensure that the investor has enough other assets to insulate him against loss. However, he is already insulated if he is in the proper tax bracket. On the other hand, an investor might have a $200,000 net worth and not be qualified. A widow who has just received her insurance settlement might technically qualify under a net worth requirement even though she is obviously not suitable. In short, a net worth requirement can exclude qualified investors and include unqualified investors. Its use as an alternative form of qualification in conjunction with an income requirement lessens the problems, but does not solve them.

These deficiencies of minimums and suitability tests have a very important implication: Ultimate responsibility lies with the selling agent. While that selling agent may use finite tests as guidelines in judging the appropriateness of a possible investment, the full variety of facts peculiar to the investor must be taken into consideration. Any reasonable finite test or standard will exclude the suitable and include the unsuitable. It must be the duty of the selling agent, using those tests and standards as a guide, to make a determination of suitability on a case by case basis.

Assessments

Some programs make provision for assessments beyond the amount of the original investment. Their purpose normally is to provide funds to develop discoveries made with the original investment.

It is impossible to predict in advance how much money an exploratory or balanced program will need. If such a program is very successful in its exploratory activities, it may generate substantial capital requirements that cannot be offset by cash flow in the short term.

Take an extreme example. Suppose that an oil program had made the initial oil discovery on the North Slope of Alaska. In so doing it would undoubtedly have done a tremendous service for its investors. However, large additional investments would have to be made — before pipelines into the area could start generating cash flow for the program. An assessment would be very useful.

From the program manager's point of view, an assessment is the most rational way to assure that adequate funds are available for the development of program reserves. Since the amount required is not predictable, it is best to have the capacity to assess whatever is necessary.

This obviously creates problems for investors. Whether an assessment feature is limited or unlimited, it introduces an element of uncertainty in personal investment planning that is undesirable. There is a further practical problem. Although an assessment indicates that a program is healthy, it will invariably be viewed with suspicion by investors.

It is for these reasons that program managers try to avoid assessment features. If investors don't like assessments, alternatives must be explored. The following are six alternatives:

1. Drill only in one or two-well areas (in other words, have a development program).

2. Farm out the development.

3. Use production loans.

4. Create a reserve from the original investments.

5. Lease equipment.

6. Sell assets.

The first solution is the most drastic and the most effective. It is also the most unwise. If a program manager confines himself to one and two-well prospects on small acreage blocks, he may be condemning his program to poor performance.

The second alternative is to have the development done by others. If properly handled, this approach can be useful, but there is a basic problem. It is never wise to be in a position that requires a particular course of action. If the program manager is forced to farm out to others, he may create a buyer's market. It is always best to be able to walk away from a potential purchaser if the terms aren't right. A program manager who has an assessment feature has a stronger bargaining position than one who does not.

The third possibility is to use production loans. If a program has proven reserves that are being sold, it can borrow money against them. That money can be used for development in other areas. This approach also can be useful — within limits. The first limitation is that borrowing power may not be equal to the capital need. A second problem is that repayment of loans delays the time that income can be distributed back to investors.

The program manager can create a reserve for development out of the initial investment. Such a step is mandatory for any prudent manager, but it too has difficulties. The percentage to be held in reserve is an arbitrary figure that will either be too high or too low. In either case, it will tend to reduce the writeoff in the first year by keeping a significant portion of the initial investment in cash.

The need for development funds can also be reduced by leasing equipment. An important part of the expenditures for productive wells is tangible. With proven production, it may be possible to lease rather than buy that equipment.

Perhaps the most obvious way to finance development is to sell other assets. It might be desirable just to sell some productive wells to pay for development in a promising area.

A program manager without an unlimited assessment power may use all six of these options to some degree. Although he would undoubtedly prefer to assess, most investors have a different opinion.

7

Costs and compensation

IT may be a mistake to discuss costs and compensation in oil program investments. In the absence of adequate performance reporting by the industry, there may be a temptation to judge the desirability of a program by its costs and management compensation.

The oil program business is like any other: you generally get what you pay for. The investor should understand how much it costs for the program manager to run the program and how much he gets paid. It should be remembered, however, that the cheapest is not always the best. Analysis of oil programs on the basis of costs, management compensation or even the capacity to generate tax deductions is an exercise in futility without adequate performance information. Nevertheless, it is important to understand these matters. It would be impossible to get a clear view of oil programs without them. Unfortunately, it is not a simple area.

Perhaps an initial generalization will help. It is useful to think of oil program money in three ways:

1. The original investment prior to expenditure in actual oil operations (sales and overhead costs).
2. The expenditure of program funds in oil operations (leasing, drilling, producing, etc.).
3. Income from productive properties (incentive compensation).

In varying degrees, all program managers obtain income from investors while their money is in at least one of these three stages.

Sales and Overhead Costs

The most common charges that come directly from the investor's

65

initial investment dollar are:

1. Sales costs
2. Registration and blue sky costs
3. Exploratory overhead
4. Management overhead

The principal part of sales costs is commissions. Oil programs generally pay commissions at a rate comparable to that of mutual funds—with the exception that the rates do not decline with volume.

The investor does not normally pay commissions directly. In most instances, the management company will take a fee of some kind (in the range of 5-10%). The management company then pays the broker the agreed upon selling commission.

On occasion, a management company will pay commissions to the selling group without an immediately offsetting fee. The problem with such an arrangement is obvious: it can generate substantial expenses for the program manager with no immediate cash to cover them. Some arrangements of this kind give the appearance of being "no load." In most cases, that is a false impression. It simply means that the investor has to look harder to find out where the program manager is charging him for sales costs.

Registration and blue sky costs (those costs associated with registering oil program offerings with the Securities and Exchange Commission and the various states) can be surprisingly high. For example, a $5 million offering which is being sold in 25 states can cost in the range of $75,000. Although the management company often absorbs these costs, they are sometimes allocated to the programs covered under the registration.

Both the Securities and Exchange Commission (SEC) and the states have recently shown an increasing tendency to be stringent. The typical oil program registration statement takes 3 months to get through the SEC. The consequence is that legal costs associated with getting a program registered are high and getting higher. Indeed, the major downside limitation on the size of a program is the registration cost. It is uneconomic to register and attempt to sell a $250,000 program in interstate commerce. Legal and registration costs alone would make it unworkable.

There are two types of overhead cost associated with the management of an oil program: management overhead and exploratory overhead.

Management overhead covers those costs associated with the

management of an oil program that exclude the scientific, technical and supervisory work of an oil company. In order to channel investor's money through a program structure into the oil business, there is a type of activity that is foreign to oil companies not in the program business. Management overhead costs include registering the program, supervising its sales, planning the use of program funds, accounting, reporting and investor service.

Figures on this type of overhead are extremely difficult to obtain, but it is reasonable to estimate they are in the range of 10-15% of total sales. Of course, there is wide variability. Some programs are lower than 10% and some are much higher than 15%. The figure depends upon the size of the program, the scope of the activities of the program manager and, obviously, the program manager's ability to hold down expenses.

Exploratory overhead includes those costs directly associated with the finding, drilling, and development of prospects. It does not include the actual cost of acreage or of the drilling, testing and completing of wells. In order to get to the point of drilling a well, a considerable amount of effort must be expended. Geological studies have to be made. Appraisals of potential profit must be determined. Mineral rights (in the form of leases) must be obtained for the prospect area. Once the well is begun, continuous supervisory activities are necessary. If production is established, the wells need to be watched by technical personnel.

Like management overhead, exploratory overhead varies considerably from program to program. Again, however, a reasonable figure is in the range of 10-15%.

One further point needs to be made about exploratory overhead. It has to do with the manner in which this overhead is incurred. For independent oil operators, it is incurred internally. The normal oil investment manager has no such internal expense. What he does is reimburse overhead costs to his oil finder.

All program managers expect to recover the costs that are incurred in behalf of investors. This is usually done on a cost basis rather than for a flat fee. The intention is not to make a profit from overhead charges, but simply to be reimbursed for such expenses.

Although this approach is a fair one, it is subject to abuse if the program manager wishes to take advantage. He has access to large amounts of money, and his own corporate profitability will not be harmed in the short term by high overhead charges. It is true that overly high overhead costs will detract from performance for investors, but it takes time for that information to be developed. In the meantime, a program manager can live very well.

Perhaps this fact accounts for the variability of overhead costs between programs for management and exploratory overhead. The industry probably averages about 30% of sales for such costs with extremes running from 15% to 40%.

It is very difficult to get figures of this sort. While sales charges appear in all prospectuses and registration costs are provided in the registration statement filed with the SEC, overhead costs are not reported publicly. Some initial efforts have been made by the Oil Investment Institute to obtain such figures, but it may be several years before complete and uniform figures are available.

No matter what the refined figures turn out to be, one thing is quite clear: Oil program managers are actually running oil companies for their investors. In that process they incur substantial overhead costs. It is a significant, if subtle point, that program managers measure overhead not as a percentage of assets (like a mutual fund), but as a percentage of sales (like any operating company).

Program managers sometimes talk about dollars that "go into the ground." What they mean is the amount of money available for actual oil operations after sales, registration and overhead costs are deducted. Using the generalizations that have already been made, an average figure can be constructed. A typical $3 million program might look this way:

Initial Investment	$10,000	(100%)
Management fees (to cover sales costs)	800	(8%)
Registration Costs	100	(1%)
Management Overhead	1,500	(15%)
Exploratory Overhead	1,500	(15%)
Dollars "Going into the ground"	6,100	(61%)

Now that these estimates have been made, it is important to point out that they mean very little. To argue, for example, that a program that puts 75% into the ground is better for investors than a program that puts 65% into the ground can be a mistake. There are two reasons.

The first reason is that intelligently spent overhead can save large amounts from the dollars that go into the ground. Suppose that the program with the 65% figure has the services of highly paid, very experienced geologists, while the other program has competent, but inexperienced geologists. The disparity of 10% could easily be made up by the greater skill of more experienced geologists.

The second reason is accounting. Different companies account for costs in different ways. The 75% figure and the 65% figure may have been determined on different bases. For example, assume that program A has an internal land department while program B uses the services of land brokers. Program A will charge its land department to exploratory overhead. Program B will allocate land brokerage fees to particular prospects, thereby indicating that such costs have gone into the ground.

This implies that sales and overhead costs, taken alone, are quite often not meaningful indicators. In some instances, they can point out managers who are abusing the money entrusted to them by investors. In most cases, however, no clear conclusions can be drawn.

Funds Received From Operations

In the process of program operations, a large number of outside services are necessary. On occasion, those services can be provided by affiliates of the program manager. The following are three of the more common types as explained by selection from prospectuses:

1. Drilling —

"Theodore I. Leben is Chairman of the Board and sole stockholder of Leben. Leben in turn is the sole stockholder of the Fund which is the sole stockholder of Aaron Corporation. Accordingly, Theodore I. Leben may be deemed to be the "promoter" and "parent" of Leben, the Fund and Aaron Corporation as those terms are defined under the Securities Act of 1933. Initially, pending the completion of its own staffing, the Fund will utilize land, geographical, engineering, technical, administrative, accounting and other services of other companies (including Leben) and will pay therefor standard rates similar to charges of others in the oil and gas industry.

"Leben is also engaged in the oil and gas business as a drilling contractor. It is anticipated that Leben will drill wells as a drilling contractor for the partnerships and that profits may, therefore, be realized by Leben as a drilling contractor. The charges which Leben will make for such services shall be equivalent to those made by reasonably prudent

drilling contractors in the area having the same experience and standards as Leben."
Natural Resources Fund, Inc. Prospectus of August 20, 1969, page 17.

2. Well Operations —

"Compensation of Operator

"MAY will serve as Manager and General Partner of both the Program Partnership and the Drilling Partnerships.

"For such managerial services, MAY will be reimbursed for a reasonable portion of its Administrative Overhead, based upon the time spent and the extent of the use of the personnel and facilities involved, for the various activities of MAY, and will receive a Program Management Fee of 10% of all subscriptions paid to the program, which will be charged to Participants as "non-Capital Costs" in the Drilling Partnerships.

"MAY, as Partnership Operator of the Drilling Partnerships, will also receive monthly per-well charges which will vary, depending on depth, from $75 to $200 for each producing well and from $500 to $1,750 for each drilling well. These rates are 50% higher for Southern Louisiana wells and 100% higher for Canadian wells. These per-well charges will be charged to Participants as Non-Capital Costs when charged at drilling well rates, and as a "Lifting Cost" to be shared by the parties in the same ratio as revenues are shared when charged at producing well rates."
May Series A Drilling Program Prospectus of September 8, 1970, page 3.

3. Turnkey Services —

"The General Partner may contract for exploratory or development projects with a general contractor on a fixed price basis. Such fixed price, which will be determined prior to commencement of the project, may include the general contractor's estimate of the direct costs and expenses of the work plus an allowance for overhead, risks, other contingencies and profit. The general contractor will realize profits to the extent that the fixed price exceeds the costs of doing the work but will incur losses to the extent that such costs are greater than the price. The fixed price charged by any general contractor which is an affiliate of the General Partner must in all cases be competitive with prices customary in the industry, taking into account the special circumstances of each case."
Prospectus of Petro-Lewis Funds, Inc., August 6, 1970, page 9.

This is a sensitive area. It is particularly dangerous because of the conflict of interest problems. There is always a possibility in such arrangements that the investor will not be fairly treated.

The ability to generate business for an affiliated company may be a major motivation for some independent oil companies to enter the program business. A drilling contractor, for example, might very much appreciate the opportunity to have a built-in market for its services.

The built-in market may allow the program manager to charge less for its incentive compensation. Of course, it also provides an opportunity to get the investor coming and going. Under such circumstances, it is particularly important that the program manager have a first rate reputation in the industry.

There are two possible solutions to the problems inherent in self-dealing. The first is more meaningful disclosure on a uniform basis. The second is simply to require that all services provided by affiliated companies be at cost. In that case, all compensation would be in the form of management fees and incentive compensation. Since self-dealing can provide significant profits to a program manager no matter what his performance, the second alternative is clearly preferable.

Incentive Compensation

For most program managers, the principal source of income is incentive compensation. Although there is a great variety of ways in which such payment can be taken, the common element is that the manager generally gets paid more as he performs better. In most instances, although not all, some form of interest is provided in the income from program properties or in the program itself.

There are eight different forms of incentive compensation: front end interests, overriding royalties, net profit interests, working interests after payout, disproportionate cost sharing, functional allocation, disproportionate risk taking, and percentage of surrender value.

Front End Interests

The Petro-Search Income Program Prospectus of June 7, 1971 describes a typical front end interest arrangement:

"Compensation. The Management Company, which will operate the business of the limited partnerships, will be reimbursed for technical, administrative and overhead expenses (including salaries of officers of the General Partner and of the Management Company) by the limited partnerships, and will receive 10% of all moneys paid to each limited partnership by the Investors as a management fee for conducting and managing the affairs of each limited partnership. All underwriting commissions will be paid by the Investors. See "Compensation" herein.
"Participation in Costs and Revenues. The Investors will receive all of the income of the limited partnerships, and will bear all of the costs of the limited partnerships. The Investors will also receive any income realized from the use of limited partnership funds pending allocation thereof. The Management Company will, however, purchase 5% of each of the properties and projects of the limited partnerships, and consequently will receive 5% of all income and will bear 5% of all costs of such properties and projects."

In this instance, Petro-Search is taking a 10% front-end fee. It invests 5% with the program and keeps the other 5% to pay corporate income taxes created by the fee. Although the company could benefit even from a poor program, it is clear that the 5% interest is worth more if the program as a whole is more successful. This approach creates an identity of interest since the program manager invests his fee along with investors.

Overriding Royalty

An overriding royalty is a percentage of the gross income. A simple description is included in the Prudential Funds, Inc. prospectus of July 18, 1969:

"The Company shall receive at the wellhead out of Participant's undivided interest in every oil and gas leasehold on overriding royalty interest which shall bear the same relationship to 3/32nds of all oil, gas and casinghead gas produced and saved from the leasehold as Participant's working interest bears to the total working interest of the Program therein."

The owner of an overriding royalty is not required to invest funds along with the program. It is just a leasehold interest that gives the manager a percentage claim on any dollars that the programs earn.

Net Profits Interests

Under a net profits arrangement, the investor is required to put up all the costs just as he does with an overriding royalty. The principal difference is that an override is a percentage of gross income while a net profits interest is a percentage of net income. This implies that a 10% overriding royalty is more valuable than a 10% net profits interest.

There is a complication. While gross income from a leasehold is easy to determine, there can be considerable ambiguity as to what net profits are.

The following is a definition of "net operating profits" from the American Minerals Fund, Inc., Prospectus of March 17, 1970:

"Net Operating Profits — The gross receipts attributable to the sale of oil and gas or sale of any lease or other property less all costs and expenses paid with respect thereto (including property, production and sales taxes) provided the following items shall not be regarded as such costs and expenses: Expenditures made to acquire and develop any property; contributions made to others for drilling wells in the vicinity of Limited Partnership property; interest paid on money borrowed to acquire any capital asset; rentals paid on lease and well equipment installed on any lease; income taxes; and allowances for depletion, depreciation and amortization. And, provided further, that the following items shall be disregarded in determining such gross receipts: Contributions including those received from others toward the drilling of a well on Limited Partnership property and amounts received from the sale of any asset up to the amount of the Federal Income Tax adjusted cost basis of the asset sold."

Under this kind of definition, which is not uncommon in the industry, net operating profits are different from a normal intuition as to what it might be. The result is that overriding royalties and net operating profits are closer in value than it may seem.

Working Interest After Payout

In a working interest after payout arrangement, sometimes called a reversionary interest, the program manager receives a percentage of the property after the investor's cost has been paid out. The program manager must then pay his pro rata share of all additional costs associated with the property. The Inexco Oil & Gas Funds,

Ltd. Prospectus of April 29, 1970 describes their compensation as follows:

"Under the Operating Contract, a partnership receives income from the production of wells on each lease until it has recovered acquisition, drilling, completion and operating costs in the lease, less any third party cash contributions made toward the drilling of any wells on the lease. Thereafter, the Operating Agent will pay 25% of additional costs and will receive 25% of production revenue, subject only to its proportionate share of royalties and other lease burdens that existed on the date the lease was committed to a partnership... If, prior to the recovery by the partnership of all its costs in the lease, a lease is sold by a partnership to a party other than the Operating Agent, the Operating Agent will receive in lieu of the interest described above, 25% of the proceeds from such sale in excess of acquisition, drilling, completion and operating costs incurred with respect to such lease not recovered through third party cash contribution and production revenue received from such lease."

The difference between a net profits interest and a working interest after payout is that the net profits owner gets a share of profits while the reversionary interest owner gets a share of the property. It is for that reason that a reversionary interest holder must make additional investments in the property, if they are necessary, while the net profits holder does not.

There is one feature common to net profits interests and reversionary interests that is important to understand. Both are geared to the concept of payout. Payout is reached when all the investor's costs are recovered. The key issue lies in determining how payout is to be defined. Under most circumstances, it is done on a lease or drilling block basis. That is, the program manager earns his compensation when the investor's costs for the lease or drilling block have been recovered.

This implies that the program manager will acquire an interest in the successful acreage. It does not imply that he will start earning money only when the investor has received all of his money back. However, like all incentive compensation, the rewards go up as performance improves.

Disproportionate Cost Sharing

In a disproportionate cost sharing arrangement, the program manager and the investor share all costs on a set basis while the sharing of income is on a basis more favorable to the program manager. The Clinton Oil Company Prospectus of October 1, 1970 explains their system:

"Participants pay 75% of Venture Fund expenditures and Clinton pays the other 25%. For their respective interests, the Participants and Clinton each will receive a 50% interest. However, Clinton receives 10% of the Venture Fund as a management fee, payable as Venture Fund expenditures are made. The general effect of the Program, since Clinton will pay 25% of Venture Fund expenditures and receive back 10% of the Venture Fund as a management fee or a net of 7½%, is that Participants will receive a 50% interest for paying 82½% of costs while Clinton will receive a 50% interest for paying 17½% of the costs and administering the Program."

Again, the manager acquires a direct interest along with investors. In a sense, disproportionate cost sharing is just a front-end interest added onto the program manager's proportionate share.

Functional Allocation

Functional allocation is a specialized form of disproportionate cost sharing. The basic format is for the investor to put up the non-capitalized costs while the manager puts up the capitalized costs. They then share revenues either according to a predetermined formula or pro rata to their contributions. Since there are no capitalized costs on dry holes, the manager invests only when oil or gas has been found.

The Serio Drilling Program, Ltd. Prospectus of July 31, 1970 describes their functional allocation system:

"Participants (including, in their individual capacities, SERIO, its officers, directors, associated and affiliated parties, who may subscribe to the Program on the same basis as other parties) will, through the Program Partnership, bear Program costs which under current law are deductible for Federal income tax purposes in the year of expenditure ("Non-Capital Costs"); these costs will include the compensation and reimbursement (discussed above) paid to SERIO for its administrative and managerial services, other than per-well charges on producing wells. Expenditures which, under current Federal income tax purposes ("Capital Costs") will be borne by SERIO. Costs of lease acquisition and equipment on productive wells are thus borne by SERIO as Capital Costs; such costs, where related to abandoned, non-productive wells or leases, are borne by Participants as deductible Non-Capital Costs, who accordingly will bear all costs of non-productive wells. Revenues, and costs of production and marketing (including per-well charges paid SERIO on producing wells ("Lifting Costs") will be shared between Participants and SERIO on a Drilling Block by Drilling Block basis, in the ratio of their respective Non-Capital and Capital Costs expended in connection with the Drilling Block. However, SERIO's share of aggregate Program revenues will be greater than its share of aggregate Program expenditures, since expenditures related to totally unproductive Drilling Blocks will not be taken into account in revenue division."

The effect of this arrangement is to increase the tax writeoffs available to investors. Some program managers indicate that they can provide a 100% writeoff in the first year. Primarily because of its ability to maximize writeoff, the use of functional allocation systems has increased in the last several years.

Disproportionate Risk Taking

The functional allocation system of Serio Drilling Program, Ltd. could also be described as a disproportionate risk taking arrangement. This is so because the program manager is able to buy into all productive properties without having to pay a share of the dry holes.

A different way of obtaining disproportionate risk taking is described in the IDS/McCulloch Oil Exploration Program - 1970 Prospectus of March 11, 1970:

"The wells for which the cost of drilling is charged to the accounts of the Participants are termed 'Participants' Wells,' and those for which such cost is charged to the General Partners are termed 'General Partners' Wells.' The right to designate any proposed well as a Participants' Well or General Partners' Well is vested solely in the General Partners. It is anticipated that the designation of a well as a 'Participants' Well' or 'General Partners' Well' will correspond to whether the well would be classified respectively as 'exploratory' or 'developmental' under industry practice. . .

"The costs of Participants' Wells, including operating costs, incurred by the Participants are accumulated on a Drilling Block basis. The Participants will be credited with all production from the Participants'

Wells drilled on a particular Drilling Block and the Partnership's share of proceeds, if any, from farmed-out wells (wells drilled and completed without costs to the Partnership) drilled on such Drilling Block, until the Participants have recovered all of the costs which have been charged to their capital accounts with respect to such Participants' Wells ('Participants' Payout'). After Participants' Payout occurs with respect to a Drilling Block, all costs of and proceeds from the Participants' Wells and farmed-out wells on the Drilling Block will be shared 60% by the Participants and 40% by the General Partners.

"With respect to General Partners' Wells drilled by the Partnership, the General Partners will be credited with all proceeds from all such wells drilled by the Partnership until they have recovered all costs charged to them with respect to such General Partners' Wells ('General Partners' Payout'). After General Partners' Payout has occurred, all further costs of the Partnership and all proceeds of the Partnership (except for costs and income with respect to farmed-out wells and Participants' Wells located on a Drilling Block as to which Participants' Payout has not occurred) are shared 60% by the Participants and 40% by the General Partners."

Although rather complicated, IDS/McCulloch's approach is quite interesting. It appears to accomplish the objective of compensating the program manager by allowing him to benefit from the risk reduction achieved by participant expenditures in exploratory areas.

Percentage of Surrender Value

An unusual form of incentive compensation is to pay the program manager a percentage of the surrender value. Since a high surrender value should indicate good performance, this fee arrangement must be regarded as incentive compensation.

The Canadian American Resources Fund, Inc. Prospectus of May 27, 1970 reads as follows:

"Can-Am will receive an annual management fee of 2¼% based on the Cash Liquidating Value of each Partnership. Such fee will be charged twice each year, in May and in November, and will be 1⅛% of the Cash Liquidating Value as then computed for each Partnership. For purposes of calculating of the management fee only, Cash Liquidating Value will not include cash on hand which represents original capital of the Partnership not yet expended, but will include any cash distributed as income to Investors since the last determination date. Such management fee is payable only out of revenues resulting from Partnership operations."

This compensation method is similar to an overriding royalty or net profits interest in that it requires no investment by the program manager. It is quite different, however, because it is based upon a valuation of the program as a whole.

Comparing Overhead and Compensation

A number of attempts have been made to compare oil programs on the basis of how much they cost and how much they charge. There is both an advantage and a danger in such studies.

The advantage is that programs that are wholly unreasonable can be weeded out. A program that takes in excess of a 20% overriding royalty does not deserve investor attention. Neither does a program whose management and exploratory overhead is 40%.

Within reasonable limits, however, comparisons can be danger-ous. Consider the final comments of Thad Thomas in a paper com-paring various incentive compensation arrangements:

"Thus, both tangible/intangible sharing and carried interest plans have merit from the investor's point of view. BUT this generalization does not serve as a blanket condemnation for all other sharing arrangements for all times. Many other considerations are necessary in drilling fund analysis. Initial charges, turnkey drilling profits, well operating fees and various accounting treatments can materially affect the investor's over-all return as can that all-important factor, management's ability to find oil. The purpose here is not to condemn over-ride funds, net profits-interest funds, or any other type of fund. The point is that, *other things being equal,* the investor's position is generally superior in either a tangible/intangible sharing arrangement or a carried interest plan than in any other type."[1]

The problem is that other things are rarely equal. At least four strong cautionary measures must be recognized before such con-clusions can have any validity at all.

[1] Thad W. Thomas, *Financial Analysis of the Common Drilling Fund Sharing Arrangements (From the Investor's Point of View),* p. 11.

1. A comparison of particular features in programs A and B is useless without total information on costs and compensation. Program A may cost the investor less for incentive compensation but be much higher in overhead costs. It is the total package, not a particular feature, that may make one program more desirable than another.

2. Comparisons should be of particular programs, not types of costs and incentive. For example, Thad Thomas' study concludes that, as a compensation type, overriding royalties are less desirable than other forms. What his paper does not indicate is that the ⅛ override figure that he uses is substantially higher than the industry average override of 3/32.

3. Comparisons of incentive compensation arrangements can be misleading because of the need to make assumptions. The compensation figures must be used on a consistent set of values for finding, developing and producing oil. Those values must be assumed.

The problem is that there is a wide variety of reasonable assumptions. Different incentive arrangements may appear more or less desirable—depending upon the assumptions.

A simple example would be to compare a 3/32 overriding royalty and a 20% net profits interest. The override would probably be more desirable in an exploratory program than a development program, while the opposite would be true of the net profits interests.

4. The quality of management is such an important feature that other types of comparison pale in usefulness. In the absence of adequate performance information, the investor should be studying the record and reputation of the management—not the particulars of its program.

8

Performance reporting

A COMPARATIVE analysis of oil programs is an exceedingly difficult task. Neither analysts nor investors currently have any reasonable method for making a rational comparison of performance. This is the case primarily because of the total inadequacy of current performance reporting practices. Until substantial changes are made, it will be impossible to obtain meaningful performance information on an industry-wide basis.

The Present System

The Apache Corporation Prospectus of January 11, 1971 includes the following language:

"What results have been achieved by Apache in its oil and gas exploration activity?
"Since 1956 Apache managed programs have drilled 1307 gross wells, 909 net wells. Of the net wells 325 produced commercial quantities of oil, 138 gas, and 446 were dry. The ratio of productive wells was 50.9%.
"The table below summarizes the total wells drilled by each program through December 31, 1969. Also included is a payout table for each program on a one unit basis. Shown are the total expenditures including operating expenses and all fees paid to Apache and the Program revenue before subtracting operating expenses but after deducting Apache's royalty and net profits interests. Future income from sales, if any, of oil and gas remaining to be produced are not included."

The table referred to includes detailed information. It reports two things: statistics (the success ratio) and cash flow. Every program manager is required to report this information in his "prior activities" section.

Well statistics report the number of wells drilled and indicate how many were productive and how many dry. A distinction is made between gross wells and net wells. Gross wells are the total number of wells in which the program manager participates. Net wells are equal to the sum of the leasehold interest in gross wells. For example, suppose that a program takes a 25% interest in four wells. On a gross well basis, it drills four wells. On a net well basis, it drills one well (because $4 \times .25 = 1$). The net well figure is more meaningful because it reflects the actual participation of the manager. It does not, however, distinguish by the cost or profitability of a well. A $20,000 producer and a $1-million dry hole yield a 50% success ratio.

Cash flow is the amount of money produced by the program. The figure is prior to any expenses and reflects total income of any kind. Also reported are total expenditures by the program. By comparing these two figures, it is hoped that an indication of the program's success can be obtained.

Statistics

The shortcomings of statistics as a reporting tool can best be illustrated through an example. Suppose that program A and program B have both raised and invested $1 million. With that money, each drills 10 wells. Program A has 8 successful wells and 2 dry holes. Program B has 2 successful wells and 8 dry holes. Which is the better program?

The answer is that there is no way of telling with this kind of information. The only significance of the figures is that program B probably drills more exploratory wells than does program A.

It is possible that all of program A's wells were marginal. A marginal well is one which has petroleum reserves, but in small quantities. With this kind of well, program A might have found only 50¢ in value for every $1 invested. Program B, on the other hand, might have found substantial value in its 2 wells that easily paid for the 8 dry holes. The opposite situation could also arise. Program B's 2 wells could both be marginal, while some or all of program A's wells might be highly profitable.

Sometimes the statistics reported distinguish between exploratory and development wells. That distinction is useful, but does not overcome the basic problem that statistics have no relationship to underlying values. Commenting on this problem, Petroleum Research Consultants concludes:

"The staff of Petroleum Research Consultants, Inc. feels that drilling fund success ratios do not yield sufficiently useful information to merit detailed analysis on a yearly basis. There are several reasons:

"(1) *There is no consistently applied standard for determining the status of a wildcat well:* A step-out well one mile from the nearest production is called a "wildcat," but so is a rank exploratory well located 25 miles from the nearest known field; funds which drill step-out wildcats should logically achieve higher success ratios than rank wildcatters, but prospectuses do not distinguish the risky wildcats from the not-so-risky wildcats.

"(2) *Scientific success (a completed well) does not indicate economic success (a profitable well).* The profitability of most wells cannot be determined for several years, so mere productivity seldom insures profitability. A fund with a 30% overall success ratio could be tremendously profitable while one with a 95% ratio could be only marginally profitable.

"(3) *Dual completions are sometimes counted as two completed wells when computing success ratios.* This distorts the averages.

We feel that any oil company management (fund company or otherwise) with a business-like approach to diversified oil exploration and the ability to prudently evaluate risks will on average, over a period of five or more years—achieve a wildcat success ratio of approximately 5%-15% and a development well success ratio of 70%-80%. Year to year fluctuations outside those ranges are a function of risk, not management ability."[1]

The consequence is clear. Since success ratios say nothing about the underlying values of a program, they have no bearing upon the evaluation of performance. The statistics section of an oil program prospectus will only tell the investor what he should already know. If there is a high success ratio, the program is undoubtedly development oriented. If the ratio is low, the program is probably exploratory in nature.

[1] Drilling Fund Reports, Petroleum Research Consultants Inc., Monthly Newsletter, Vol. 1, No. 2, April 1970, pp. 1-2.

The only value of statistics is that they may weed out programs at the extremes. A zero success ratio presents obvious problems. Similarly, a 100% ratio can only mean that the program consistently drills low return prospects that no one else can justify drilling.

Cash Flow

Cash flow is more significant than statistics, but it is subject to important limitations. Again, compare program A and program B.

Program A drills its 10 prospects for fast payout oil reserves close to pipelines. Program B drills primarily for longer payout gas reserves in the Arctic. Program A is 50% paid out in 2 years; program B is 10% paid out in 2 years. Which program is better?

The answer again is that there is no way of telling from the information given. Program A looks much better after 2 years, but there is a distinct possibility that program A's wells will produce for 4 years, while those of program B will produce for 40 years.

This possibility exemplifies a problem inherent in cash flow analysis. The most important figure is not the percentage rate of cash flow. What must be understood is the difference between return of principal and return of income. The program that pays out 25% a year for 4 years and then quits, does not have a 25% rate of return. It has a 0% rate of return (on a discounted cash flow basis, it has a negative rate of return).

The prospectus reports cash flow, but it does not distinguish between principal and income. In order to make that distinction, a sophisticated petroleum reserve study would be necessary. If the reserve study were done, the results could be published in a manner more meaningful than a breakdown of cash flow between principal and income. Like statistics, cash flow information does not address itself to the critical question of underlying values.

Cash flow information does become more meaningful as time passes. If all program A's wells are fully depleted in 4 years, the cash flow information by that fourth year is highly informative. Unfortunately, there are two important complications. The first is that cash flow reports only become meaningful when the program has almost fully depleted its reserves. Until that time, the investor lacks conclusive evidence as to how his investment has performed. The second complication is that it typically takes a long time to reach the point where full depletion has occurred. Apache Corporation's 1956 program (one of the first publicly offered programs) is still distributing income to its investors.

The obvious response to this predicament is that extrapolations on the payout charts should be made. Surely, at some point in time, it must be possible to project past income into the future. After enough years have passed, this approach does have value, but it is not without problems. In notes to its payout charts, Resource Programs Institute gives the following warning:

"Interpreting Payout: An estimate of payout time obtained by dividing remaining expenditures to be recovered by average monthly receipts is apt to be misleading. This is so because:

"a) Average monthly receipts are gross receipts. Various expenses, such as operating expenses and overhead, must be deducted to obtain monthly operating income (cash flow).

"b) There is no assurance that average monthly receipts or operating income will continue at the recent level; receipts may increase or decrease. For example, an increase may result from the completion of additional wells, increased allowable production or the connection of shut-in gas wells; on the other hand, decreases with time are inevitable as reserves are exhausted.

"A more reasonable estimate of payment may be derived from the accompanying performance graphs. *Extrapolation of the curves should be used only with reservation and in a qualitative or semi-quantitative sense. Additional information plus technical judgment are required for a more meaningful estimate of payout."* (Emphasis added).[2]

The "additional information" and "technical judgment" are important. They point the way to a far more helpful evaluation approach: discounted future net income. The problem with cash flow as an evaluation method is that it looks at future net income only after the future has arrived. If projections are not made, cash flow information takes years to become meaningful. If projections are made, additional information and technical judgment are necessary. If that information and judgment are available, a value for discounted future net income (the present value) can be constructed. Discounted future net income is a far better indication of performance than is payout.

[2] A Continuing Study of Oil and Gas Drilling Programs, Resource Programs Institute, New York, N.Y.

Present Value Analysis

The purpose of present value analysis is to reach a dollar figure which can be compared to the original investment. It is simply an attempt to answer the investor's legitimate question, "How much is my investment worth?" To those unfamiliar with the oil business, it may appear ridiculous to make so much out of such a simple question. The difficulty is that petroleum reserves are not amenable to accurate evaluation until several years after they are discovered and put on production. This subject will be discussed in more detail in Chapter 9.

If the program interest has been converted to common stock in a corporation, the trading price of the stock is the present value. If an investor has converted a $10,000 investment into 2,000 shares, trading at $5.00 per share, evaluation is easy. The price of the stock is subject to fluctuation, but on any given day the investor knows exactly how he has done.

If no exchange for common stock has taken place, the investor must rely upon evaluations by the program manager or, preferably, by outside consultants. That evaluation requires two kinds of skill. First, petroleum engineers must study the reserves of the program. That study involves a highly technical analysis of the characteristics of each productive property. Second, qualified individuals must evaluate all other assets of the program. Undeveloped acreage is probably the most important asset of this kind. Placing a market value on such acreage requires intimate knowledge of the areas in which the acreage is located.

The following steps must be taken in a present value analysis:

1. Estimate future net income of proven reserves;
2. Estimate future net income of probable and possible reserves;
3. Decide upon a discount rate to bring future net income back to present value;
4. Discount future net income back to present value. The value of probable and possible reserves may be excluded entirely or reduced by some reasonable factor to allow for the uncertainty of their being only probable or possible;
5. Evaluate all of the assets of the program such as undeveloped leasehold, cash, or tangible assets with salvage value;
6. Add the discounted future net income to the value of all other assets.

In the event that the present value analysis is done for the purpose of computing a surrender value, oil program managers then normally multiply the figure arrived at by a multiple in the range of 66% to 80%.

In a typical present value analysis, the management of Petro-Search gives this explanation:

"1. Future net income has been discounted to present value at 7%.
  2. Reserves are included on the following basis: (a) 100% of proven reserves; (b) 75% of probable reserves; (c) 50% of possible reserves.
"3. Assets are evaluated as follows: (a) Cash—100%; (b) undeveloped leaseholds at market value; (c) drilling wells at cost.
  4. Investment required for undrilled locations subtracted from probable and possible reserves.
  5. No increase above current prices for oil. The recent 25¢/barrel increase in crude oil was not included because of political uncertainties.
  6. Gas prices include only product price increases specified in contracts already signed.
  7. Production income to date has or will be invested in development drilling and is not available for distribution.
  8. With respect to the 69-5 program additional technical work has been done on certain program properties. That work was complete after the effective date of this report. Management estimates that this work has upgraded the value of the 69-5 program by approximately 9%.
  9. This evaluation is Petro-Search's estimate of program values. It is not an offer to buy. At the present time, there is no ready market for these units."[3]

The value to investors of present value information is apparent. The knowledge that a $10,000 investment has a present value of $9,500 is far more useful than the knowledge that the $10,000 will be paid out in 6.1 years or that it has purchased a pro rata share in a program with a 27.6% success ratio.

The Effect of Statistics and Cash Flow Reporting

The Securities and Exchange Commission allows only statistics and cash flow information in the prospectus. The reason for its

3 Petro-Search, Inc., "Program Progress," December, 1970.

exclusion of present values will be discussed in the next section. Prior to that, it is appropriate to consider what effect present reporting practices have had.

The first result is that investors and analysts have had weak data upon which to make their judgments. The situation is rather like judging a common stock on the basis of the company's dividend rate and its ratio of current assets to current liabilities. This simply is not the right kind of information to make an in-depth analysis. Such data, while interesting, is only a surface indication of the underlying economic strength. The basis of an oil program's strength lies in the value of its petroleum reserves and its other assets. Without information on reserves and assets, the whole analytical process is on a weak foundation.

This weakness has led some people to judge oil programs on the basis of structure, costs and management compensation. The theory is that, in the absence of performance information, at least it may be possible to find a program that is structured in favor of the investor. Beyond that, it may well be the case that those most capable of performing structure their programs more in favor of the manager.

The tradition of statistics and cash flow reporting has had another unfortunate result. Since the "performance" section requires such data, investors have been led to judge programs by these standards. It is perfectly reasonable for uninitiated investors and dealers to believe that prospectus performance disclosures are meaningful. Certainly, if the Securities and Exchange Commission requires this information, it has the Commission's endorsement that it is useful.

This has led some programs, and particularly development programs, to sell on the basis of success ratios and early cash flow. Development programs are the best performers by those standards. It was pointed out in an earlier chapter that development programs are the least likely to make a reasonable return on investment. This means that current performance reporting practices have done a neat job of turning things upside down. The "performance" section of the prospectus makes those programs which are least capable of performing look the best.

This is not a small matter. In the last several years, development programs have outsold exploratory and balanced programs. Their indirect endorsement by the Securities and Exchange Commission has certainly helped.

The SEC Position

It would be unfair not to present the arguments made by the SEC in excluding present value information. Its position centers around two key points: Evaluation of petroleum reserves is highly inexact; and, therefore, it is possible for petroleum engineers, even those from reputable independent firms, to come up with "reasonable" values which nevertheless substantially distort the actual value of recoverable reserves.

There is no point to going into detail on the various methods of reservoir evaluation. The most important fact is that accurate evaluations are possible only after a significant amount of time has passed.

One expert in this field has observed:

"Reserves are a fluid thing and should be determined periodically. Their accuracy depends on the quality and quantity of data available. Since more information necessarily accumulates during the life of a property, the reserve estimates become correspondingly more accurate. The periods of time during which reserves are determined may be shown as:
(1) prior to drilling and development
(2) just after drilling and completion
(3) after at least one year's production data are available, the well or lease still producing its allowable
(4) when the property in question will not make its allowable and production is declining
(5) at depletion
The data are listed in the order of their accuracy."[4]

There is one distinction that should be made. Evaluation just after drilling and completion of the well is based upon volumetrics. Using test data obtained, it is possible to estimate reserves from estimates as to porosity and permeability of the rock combined with estimates of recoverability and areal extent of the reservoir. A year or two later (after production is established), reserve evaluation can be based upon production decline curves and from reservoir pressure data. Although this latter evaluation is still inexact, it is far more reliable than estimates based upon volumetric calculations. Once a well is completed, the greatest reduction in uncertainty

4 Campbell, John M., *Oil Property Evaluation,* Prentice Hall, 1959, P. 120.

occurs in the first year or two. After that, it often is a matter of successively reducing the margin of error.

Simliar problems arise in the evaluation of undeveloped lease-hold interests. The value of leases can go up or down as wells are either productive or dry in an area. Ultimately, the value of a lease will be closely related to the reserves that it contains, but it may take years to find out what those reserves are—especially if the lease is being held in the hope that others with adjacent acreage will drill test wells to prove or disprove the lease. Until that point, the value placed on the lease may depend upon the optimism or pessimism of the appraiser.

The argument of the SEC is that, in this climate of uncertainty, it is possible to mislead investors. Evaluation figures will almost certainly turn out to be wrong in the long run. The best that can be hoped is that the margin of error is small. Since the program manager wants to have high evaluation figures, he may apply pressure on the evaluation to be optimistic.

The appropriate response to this argument is to look at the alternatives. While admitting the inaccuracy of present value analysis, it must be emphatically pointed out that statistics and cash flow are the only other data available—and they are far worse than present value analysis as an indication of performance. At the same time, it is important to recall that value analysis can be reasonably close. As Campbell says:

"Even a casual examination of the foregoing reserve methods indicates that calculation of reserves depends upon a number of independent but potentially inexact methods. Because of this, one may assume that reserve calculations are generally unreliable. This is not the case.

"In the first place, the fact that a number of methods and correlations exist gives one the opportunity to develop answers that are relatively consistent with the available facts and the methods tried. Estimating reserves is analogous to playing poker, and the use of several approaches simply increases the odds of success. Failure to use several methods when possible, whether through laziness or carelessness, is inexcusable. If, in addition, one examines the data with integrity and applies the intangible called good judgment, the accuracy of the results is often surprising."[5]

[5] *Ibid.,* p. 148

An Approach

The Business Standards of the Oil Investment Institute require that, "To the extent permitted by law and pertinent regulatory authorities, each program should periodically provide its investors with value information in a standardized manner . . . Such information, based upon engineering reports prepared by a qualified independent petroleum engineer, shall be provided to each investor in an oil program within 90 days after the close of the second full calendar year of the program's existence, as of the close of such year, and promptly after any material change in the information so provided."

This standard is a reasonable one and provides a better value reporting system than any now in use. It has three important features:

1. Independent appraisal
2. Time lag of 2-3 years
3. Periodic updates

The reason for requiring an independent appraisal should be obvious. It is hard enough for engineers to provide accurate estimates without having a vested interest in the outcome. Evaluations by employees of the sponsor may be excellent, but they can be subject to suspicion. A program manager will normally want high values to report because they will help future sales. An employee of the program manager may be prone to be overly optimistic.

A time lag of 2 to 3 years is very important. By that time, it is reasonable to believe that program wells will have some production history. With that history, far more accurate evaluations can be made. Prior to that time, evaluations may be meaningless. It may not be possible to avoid giving estimates before 2 to 3 years because investors and brokers almost invariably regard the claim that it is not possible to evaluate program interests early as highly suspicious. They fear that the program manager is hiding something; but it definitely is desirable if the resulting numbers are to have any real significance.

The final requirement of the Business Standards is that the evaluation be updated periodically. While it would be too expensive to get independent evaluations periodically, the program manager can update the evaluation "based upon" earlier independent appraisals. Presumably, the margin of error in each periodic appraisal would be smaller than the last one.

90

9

Taxes and investment analysis

THE subjects of oil and gas taxation and program investment analysis are so interrelated that it is appropriate to consider them together. Although taxation can be a complicated subject, there is no need in this discussion to go into complex detail.

Taxes must be considered in three areas: intangibles, depletion and capital gains. Investment analysis will be primarily based upon the use of present value information.

Intangibles and Other Deductible Costs

There is no doubt that the treatment of intangible drilling costs is the most important tax advantage available to oil program investors. It is the basis upon which most of the deductions from current income become possible. Section 1.612-4 of the Internal Revenue Code is the source for this treatment:

"Section 1.612-4. Charges to capital and to expense in case of oil and gas wells.—(a) Option with respect to intangible drilling and development costs. In accordance with the provisions of section 263(c), intangible drilling and development costs incurred by an operator . . . in the development of oil and gas properties may at his option be chargeable to capital or to expense. This option applies to all expenditures made by an operator for wages, fuel, repairs, hauling, supplies, etc., incident to and necessary for the drilling of wells and the preparation of wells for the production of oil or gas. Such expenditures have for convenience been termed intangible drilling and development costs.

They include the cost to operators of any drilling or development work
... done for them by contractors under any form of contract, including
turnkey contracts. Examples of items to which this option applies are,
all amounts paid for labor, fuel, repairs, hauling, and supplies, or any
of them, which are used—

(1) In the drilling, shooting, and cleaning of wells,
(2) In such clearing of ground, draining, road making, surveying,
    and geological works as are necessary in preparation for the
    drilling of wells, and
(3) In the construction of such derricks, tanks, pipelines, and other
    physical structures as are necessary for the drilling of wells and
    the preparation of wells for the production of oil or gas.

In general, this option applies only to expenditures for those drilling
and developing items which in themselves do not have a salvage value.
For the purpose of this option, labor, fuel, repairs, hauling, supplies, etc.,
are not considered as having a salvage value, even though used in connection with the installation of physical property which has a salvage
value. Included in this option are all costs of drilling and development
undertaken (directly or through a contract) by an operator of an oil and
gas property whether incurred by him prior or subsequent to the formal
grant or assignment to him of operating rights . . ."

In addition to intangibles, certain other expenses such as management fees, overhead costs and condemned acreage are also
deductible. In a typical program, the total of all deductible items
available as writeoffs to investors averages between 60% and 100%
of the original investment.

Not all expenditures incurred by an oil program are deductible.
Some must be capitalized and written off over a period of years.
The most important items in this category are tangibles and invest-
ments in productive leases.

Tangibles are items which have salvage value. They are primarily
the costs associated with the completion of a productive well. The
cost of a well can be broken down into two broad categories: dry
hole costs and completion costs. Dry hole costs are the expenses
necessary to drill a hole to the desired depth. They must be incurred whether the well is dry or productive. This type of expense
is intangible in nature because it generates no assets with salvage
value. When the well reaches total depth, testing is done to determine whether petroleum is present in commercial quantities. If the
well appears successful, it will be completed. Completion of a well
involves a substantial investment in production casing and such

equipment as pumping units, tanks, separators and the like. All of these are tangibles and must be capitalized.

In the event that production is established, the cost of the acreage must be capitalized. Of course, if the acreage is proven to be worthless, then the investment can be written off. Until the time that the acreage is actually dropped, however, the original investment in land cannot be written off.

The amount and timing of the deductible costs available to investors is dependent upon a variety of factors. Since deductions relate directly to tax savings and since tax savings are central to program performance, it is worthwhile to consider several factors that affect deductions. The following is a list of some of the more important aspects to bear in mind:

1. Deductibility in income programs,
2. Production loans,
3. Leasing,
4. Tangible—Intangible sharing arrangements,
5. Undeveloped leasehold inventory.

Since income programs do not drill wells, they do not provide significant tax savings. The purchase price of productive properties must be capitalized. The "tax aspects" section of the Petro-Lewis Oil Income Program Prospectus of July 28, 1970 explains this point:

"Intangible Deductions not a Material Factor: Investors in other oil and gas programs, the principal functions of which are exploratory or development drilling, can frequently deduct as intangible drilling and development costs a substantial portion of their investment. The Oil Income Program Partnerships, however, will expend substantially all of their funds for the acquisition of producing properties plus the equipment thereon. Accordingly, the major part of a Limited Partner's investment will be required to be capitalized by the Partnerships as cost of the producing properties acquired and the deduction for intangible costs is not expected to be material in amount."

This means that an investor who wants tax savings should not buy income programs or drilling programs which invest a substantial portion of their funds in productive properties.

Program managers frequently use production loans to finance development on discovery acreage. Using the reserves already proven as collateral, the manager can drill development wells with borrowed money. This not only avoids the need for an assessment, but it tends to increase write-offs.

Suppose that a 70% write-off has been achieved for the investor in the first year. The remaining 30% is invested in capitalized items such as completion equipment and productive leases. Using the reserves found in the first year as collateral, additional intangible deductions can be created with borrowed funds.

Obviously, this approach will not work if no reserves are found or if no development is necessary. In a reasonably successful program, however, deductions totaling 90% to 100% of the original investment can be reached in a 2 to 3-year period.

Another method of increasing deductions is to lease rather than purchase tangibles. The lease payments are deductible and overcome the need for a direct investment in capitalized equipment. By doing so, depreciation in future years is lost, but the net effect is to increase current deductions by allocating more program funds in the direction of intangible expenses.

The functional allocation sharing arrangement discussed in Chapter VII is a common way of increasing deductions for investors. For an agreed upon share of revenues, the program manager pays all tangible costs while the investor pays all intangible costs.

The result is that first year deductions to investors frequently amount to 90% to 100% of the original investment. This means that the manager may have to pay substantial capitalized costs.

That disadvantage from the manager's point of view is offset by two facts. First, the program manager frequently takes a higher portion of revenues than he pays of costs. He might, for example, invest 30% of the funds for 50% of the revenues. Second, he only invests in completing productive wells. His risk, therefore, is not a dry hole risk. The danger is that he will complete non-commercial or marginal wells where the sharing arrangement precludes recovery of completion costs.

Tax deductions, taken alone, cannot justify an oil program investment. The fact that production loans, leasing or functional allocation increase deductions does not presumptively justify using those techniques. Tax savings are a factor in the economics of oil programs, but there are other important elements. Even the tax savings might not justify the interest rate on production loans or the risk of drilling dry holes with borrowed money. Leasing can be expensive and may cost investors money in the long run for the sake of immediate deductions. A functional allocation system may or may not be fair—depending upon the division of revenues relative to the sharing of costs. Functional allocation may also force the managers to make cash commitments in excess of its capacity. It also interposes a conflict of interest between investors and managers in the decision to complete or not to complete marginal wells.

Since investors generally tend to buy for tax savings more than for capital appreciation, program managers are frequently tempted to maximize deductions. In the process of maximizing deductions, they can damage long run profitability in a manner that completely offsets short-term tax savings. This is a conflict that all managers must live with. Perhaps an example involving the problem of carrying undeveloped leasehold will clarify what is meant.

One of the soundest principles of exploration is that a substantial acreage position is necessary to maximize the chance of success. There are two reasons. First, the high risk character of exploration requires broad exposure. The odds are against an operator who doesn't have a large number of possible prospects. Second, it is pointless to make the large expenditures necessary in exploration and then not control substantial acreage in the area if a discovery is made.

The major oil companies follow this pattern. They acquire large acreage positions in a potential area and begin the process of exploration—either directly or by farming out to others.

There is an important reason why it may be difficult for program managers to follow this proven approach. Undeveloped leases must be carried at cost. Until the acreage is condemned (or the owner surrenders the leases), investments in lease acquisition cannot be written off. Since it may take years to prove or disprove the value of acreage in exploratory areas, there is a tendency to carry the initial investment for a relatively long time. This puts two principles in conflict: to maximize deductions, undeveloped leasehold inventory should be kept at a minimum; to maximize possible exploratory success, undeveloped leasehold inventory should be substantial.

The response to this dilemma is that the value of tax savings must be weighed against the cost in possible revenues. Although tax savings may be the principal motivation for investors, the investment is poor if no value is created. Tax savings are an important element in determining profitability, but they have to be accompanied by the creation of value. If they are not, the investor might just as well have given his money to a charity.

Depletion

The depletion allowance is undoubtedly the best known tax shelter available to oil investors. However, the publicity generated on the subject may have created the wrong impression for oil programs. Although statutory depletion is an important tax shelter, it does not play nearly as significant a role with oil programs as does the treatment of intangibles.

Statutory depletion is a method of sheltering part of the income from a productive property. It amounts to a deduction from gross income of 22% (but not to exceed net income by 50%). The concept of depletion is quite like depreciation. It is a non-cash expense item that gives recognition to the lessening value of an asset over time. At some point, production from a reservoir will decline to zero. Depletion charges recognize that abandonment comes nearer each year.

The difference between depreciation and statutory depletion is that statutory depletion allows deductions in excess of cost. Depreciation charged against a building cannot exceed the amount invested. Charges for depletion can, and frequently do, exceed the amount invested in the lease.

It is important to distinguish between statutory depletion and cost depletion. Cost depletion can be analogized to straight line depreciation. Charges are based upon withdrawals from the reservoir in relation to total reservoir capacity. Consequently, only statutory depletion provides a tax shelter.

For those programs where interests are held through the production phase without conversion or redemption, the depletion allowance is a valuable additional incentive.

Capital Gains

The treatment of capital gains in an oil program investment is no different from any other capital gain. However, there is one area that may cause confusion. It concerns the basis from which capital gains are determined.

Suppose that an investor has $10,000 in a program. Within two years, he has deducted 90% of that investment from his taxable income. He then sells his investment for $9,000.

It may appear that he can claim a capital loss of $1,000 because he sold the investment for $1,000 less than he paid for it. That is not the case. The reason is that the tax deductions reduce the investor's "basis." In 2 years, the investor has claimed, for income tax purposes, that he has lost 90% of his investment (a loss of $9,000). Consequently, the Internal Revenue Service views the investor's basis as $10,000 less $9,000. The investor must pay a capital gains tax on the difference between $1,000 and $9,000.

The obvious advantage is that the losses are deductible against regular income (taxed at 40% to 60%) while the capital gain is subject to a lower rate (probably 25%). The investment has also deferred the payment of a tax until the program interest is actually sold.

After Tax Cost

There are three different ways of looking at an investor's "cost" in an oil program investment. The Internal Revenue Service's understanding of cost for tax purposes has just been discussed. The most obvious, and least useful figure for cost, is the amount of the original investment. For the purpose of meaningful economic analysis, the use of after tax cost is necessary.

After tax cost is the amount of the original investment, plus any assessments, less the tax savings created by the investment. To determine after tax cost, the following must be understood:

1. Assume that investor X has invested $10,000 in an oil program.
2. Investor X is consistently in the 50% tax bracket.
3. Deductions allocable to his interest are: 70% in the first year; 20% in the second year; 10% in the third year.

From this information, it can be concluded that the investor has reduced his taxes by $5,000 over the three-year period. That conclusion is based upon the following reasoning:

1. Assume that X is the investor's taxable income before deductions created by the oil program.

97

2. Then,
   X — $7,000 = first year taxable income
   X — $2,000 = second year taxable income
   X — $1,000 = third year taxable income

3. At a tax rate of 50%, tax savings were:
   $ 7,000 × 50% = $3,500
   $ 2,000 × 50% = $1,000
   $ 1,000 × 50% = $ 500

Total $10,000 × 50% = $5,000 in tax savings

This same figure of $5,000 in tax savings can be reached for the investor in a simpler case. Suppose that 100% in deductions are generated the first year. Then,

Original Investment	$10,000
First year deductions (100%)	10,000
Tax rate	50%
Tax savings	$ 5,000

In practice, of course, determination of tax savings is more complicated. Deductions rarely amount to convenient round numbers. An investor's tax bracket will vary from year to year. Nevertheless, the approach is the same.

Once tax savings have been determined, it is a simple matter to find after tax cost. In the two cases just discussed, after tax cost is $5,000. This is so because $10,000 (the original investment) less $5,000 (the tax savings) equals $5,000.

In summary, after tax cost is the investor's net dollar exposure after giving recognition to tax savings. This means that an investor breaks even (before capital gains tax, if any) on his investment not at the amount of his original investment, but at the amount of his after tax cost. A ten-thousand dollar investment that buys five thousand in value and five thousand in tax savings is a break-even deal before capital gains.

Several characteristics of after tax cost should be mentioned here.

First, after tax cost can change from year to year. In the first instance just discussed, after tax cost went from $6,500 (first year) to $5,500 (second year) to $5,000 (third year). This implies that the timing of a sale of a program unit may affect profitability— even if the selling price stays the same.

Second, the after tax cost figure does not reflect the timing of tax savings. By the end of the third year, both examples showed an after tax cost of $5,000. But the second case, other things being equal, is more desirable because tax savings were created earlier—thereby giving the investor the use of his tax savings for a longer period of time.

Third, after tax cost varies from investor to investor even within the same program. Since a part of the formula is tax bracket, after tax cost is a function of each investor's taxable income. This fact is the key to why oil programs are most appropriate to high income investors. Higher income tax rates mean lower after tax costs. Lower after tax costs reduce risk and make reasonable performance easier to attain.

Investment Analysis

The subject of performance reporting was discussed in Chapter VIII. Its conclusion was that the single most important piece of information that can be provided is the present value of the reserves and assets of the program (unless, of course, surrender values or the value of exchanged stock are available). In conjunction with a figure for after tax cost, present value information provides an excellent indication of performance.

A simple but fairly accurate rule of thumb is that a manager who creates, on average, one dollar of present value for each dollar invested is doing an excellent job for his investors. While every investment has to be judged on a precise basis, this rule of thumb owes its appeal to the following kind of analysis:

Assume that an investor in the 50% tax bracket has invested $10,000 in a program. Over a three-year period he deducts $10,000 from taxable income (a 100% write-off). With that deduction, he reaches an after tax cost of $5,000.

If the investment has a present value of one dollar for each dollar invested, it is worth ten thousand dollars. With an after tax cost of $5,000, the investor is ahead by $5,000. If he sells the interest for $10,000, he will probably incur a capital gains tax of $2,500. This makes calculation of the "profit" a simple matter:

Original Investment	$10,000
Less: Tax savings	5,000
After tax cost	$ 5,000
Selling Price	$10,000
Less: After tax cost	5,000
Less: Capital gains tax	2,500
"Profit"	$ 2,500

The $2,500 profit amounts to 50% on after tax cost and 25% on the original investment.

It must be emphasized that this approach is only a useful indicator. Since it is easy to construct, it can be a convenient guide. A major deficiency is that no recognition is given to the time value of money. The timing of a hypothetical sale as well as the timing of write-offs can materially affect the rate of return on an investment. Equally as important is the fact that no recognition is given to income paid out to investors.

In order to find an investor's rate of return on his investment, it would be necessary to determine:

1. The amount and date of the original investment;
2. The amount and date of any assessments;
3. The amount and date of all write-offs;
4. The amount and date of all income;
5. The amount and date of evaluation (the present value figure);
6. The amount and date of any gains tax.

With that information, a true measure of performance can be reached.

Oil Programs and Finding Costs

It has been indicated that a dollar of present value for each dollar invested provides a good return for suitable investors. What is the likelihood that this performance will be obtained?

This is not an easy question to answer. If it can be answered with any accuracy at all, the key is in oil industry finding costs. A finding cost is the cost involved in discovering petroleum reserves. It is the amount of money spent looking for petroleum divided by the number of barrels of oil (or equivalent amounts of gas) found with

100

that expenditure. A composite industry average finding cost is determined annually.

John S. Herold, Inc., a research organization, reports the following finding costs for a barrel of oil in the United States and Canada:

Estimated Cost of Finding and Developing Petroleum[1]

Year	U.S.A. Cost Per Barrel
1969	1.90
1968	1.10
1967	.75
1966	.89
1965	.88

Appendix *D* contains a detailed study by Richard H. Roda. Its purpose is "to compare fee structure for varying degrees of success and to attempt to find the maximum net finding cost per barrel net to the investor which can be supported and still have an economically 'successful' program." Mr. Roda's analysis is worthy of careful attention.

This sort of study is subject to a variety of pitfalls. Particularly in measuring compensation, the outcome may be a function of the original model more than of the compensation arrangements studied. Nevertheless, some general idea can be developed that will provide a framework which is reasonable in relating finding costs to success.

Mr. Roda's study shows two things:

1. "If 'success' for a drilling program is defined as achieving a present worth for the investor of $1.00 per dollar invested, then the maximum finding cost (not including sponsor's fees) that can be supported is about $1.50 per barrel."

After making allowance for the manager's incentive compensation and sales costs, he concludes that a net finding cost to the investor of $2.00 per barrel is necessary.

2. Mr. Roda also concludes that sharing arrangements have little effect on the outcome. He says, "Assuming the drilling program industry operates within a finding cost range from $1.30 to $2.00 per barrel, the curves (for six of the seven incentive compensa-

[1] *Petroleum Outlook,* John S. Herold, Inc., Vol. 24, No. 2, February, 1971, p. 3.

tion arrangements studied) show remarkably little spread. In fact, the less successful the industry is, the closer the curves become. If the average base finding cost of a program is $2.00 per barrel, an investor can see no difference between fee structures 2, 3, 4, 5, 7 and 8. Whatever the fee structure of the program in which he has invested, his present worth value is 72 cents per dollar invested (plus or minus 3 cents)."

The most important figure is the $1.50 per barrel finding costs prior to management fees and incentive compensation. If that figure can be matched, investors will be given a reasonable return on investment.

It is not unreasonable to claim that oil programs can perform at this level. The John S. Herold study showed a $1.03 per barrel finding cost in the U.S. for 1964-1969. While finding costs are rising, oil programs still have room to perform well so long as they find oil at about the same cost as the industry as a whole. Of course, some programs may do better than the average and others will do worse.

10

Regulation of oil programs

THE oil program business is involved in both the securities and oil industries. The money-raising effort is securities work; the money-investing is oil business. A full discussion of oil program regulation would extend to both of those areas.

This chapter will be restricted to securities. Although state and federal involvement in the petroleum industry is substantial, an analysis of that involvement is less important to an understanding of the workings of oil programs.

There are five areas to consider:
1. The Securities and Exchange Commission (SEC)
2. State securities commissions (Blue Sky agencies)
3. National Association of Securities Dealers (NASD)
4. Oil Investment Institute (OII)
5. Future federal legislation

Securities and Exchange Commission (SEC)

Federal control of oil programs covers every public offering made in more than one state. While there is considerable ambiguity as to what constitutes a public offering, it is fair to say that almost all of the large programs are registered with the SEC. There are, however, quite a few unregistered private placements regularly sold by independent oil companies.

Oil programs come under both the Securities Act of 1933 and the Securities Exchange Act of 1934. The Securities Act of 1933 is of particular interest. That law is intended to provide adequate disclosure and is not really a "regulatory" statute at all. Its purpose, as it relates to public offerings of securities, is to provide investors with a prospectus which discloses the material features of the offering. The Securities Act of 1933 does not forbid the sales of outrageously unfair offerings; it merely requires that such offerings be fully explained.

A filing is initiated when the offeror files a registration statement on form S-1. That form requires lengthy and detailed information on such subjects as risk factors, compensation, management, conflicts of interest, prior activities, structure of the offering, underwriting arrangements, tax aspects, financial condition of the offeror and method of operation. While some of the language is standard, each registration is a major task for an attorney.

Most of the language of the registration statement constitutes the body of the prospectus. The final prospectus serves two important purposes. First, it gives investors a full description from which they can judge the merits of the investment. Second, it lays a groundwork to which the program manager is bound. He is free to structure the program as he wishes, but once his prospectus is approved, his flexibility is gone. The danger of legal sanctions should ensure that the manager will operate the program as he said he would.

It normally takes 3 months for an oil program offering to get through the SEC and become "effective." An offering is effective with the SEC only after the SEC is satisfied with the prospectus. Prior to the effective date, there is a considerable amount of legal work necessary to get the prospectus into acceptable form. Until that point, the program manager cannot sell program units. He can, on a limited basis, take indications of interest from a preliminary prospectus.

The Oil and Gas Section of the SEC is staffed by professionals who do an excellent job. To a large extent, they have succeeded in carrying out the objectives of the Securities Act of 1933. Nevertheless, there are problem areas that deserve mention. Performance reporting has been discussed in an earlier chapter and needs no further elaboration. A second difficulty is the length of time needed for review. A third and particularly distressing problem is the complexity of the typical oil program prospectus.

The growth of oil program filings in recent years has not been accompanied by a proportionate growth in the SEC's ability to process those filings. There are just not enough people at the SEC to do the work rapidly. From the date of filing to the effective date, the delay is normally 3 months. A registration by a company that has registered a similar program in the past may take less time. A complicated program that raises serious disclosure questions could take a year or more.

This delay is burdensome. It makes investment planning difficult and subjects the program manager to the danger of unrecoverable overhead. It occasionally puts the manager beyond a point where he can achieve reasonable tax savings in the current year.

While 3 months is an average, the timing for any particular program is uncertain. A prudent manager begins investigating prospects long before the effective date of the program. There must be a constant flow of potential investments, if the best possible prospects are to be acquired. Beyond the normal uncertainty as to program size, (since sales forecasts can only be approximate), the registration delay makes the timing of the program unclear. This means that the manager must review potential investments without specific knowledge as to how much he can spend nor when he will have the money. This tends to put him in a defensive posture.

Unplanned delays in registration time can pose serious problems for small program managers. The SEC can, and occasionally does, put the program manager in the position of not having anything to sell. With overhead costs running during that period, the squeeze can be very uncomfortable.

The answer to this sort of difficulty, of course, is to file early. A prudent manager should file at least 6 months in advance of his anticipated closing date. This approach makes it difficult to make rapid decisions and can discourage new companies from entering the business.

The most ironic part of the registration process is that investors do not normally read a prospectus. Prospectuses are intended to provide investors with complete information on an offering, but their complexity and length are overwhelming. The language is technical and bears the mark of being worked and reworked by assorted attorneys. The average oil program investor is a busy man with substantial income. He just doesn't have the time.

After months of intensive effort and thousands of dollars in printing and legal costs, the investor is presented with a document that he does not read. It is reasonably accurate to say that prospectuses are read by competitors, state regulators, research services, a few brokers, fewer investors and attorneys for dissident investors who later think they might sue. No one else has the time nor the ability to read and understand a typical oil program prospectus.

Blue sky agencies

Once a program is effective, the sponsor must gain permission to sell from the securities commission ("blue sky" commission) in those states where the program will be sold.

Lewis G. Mosburg explains the problem:

"Unlike many areas in which the federal government, upon entering a regulatory field, has preempted it, federal regulation of securities is concurrent with rather than exclusive of state regulation. Accordingly, an effective registration of program interests under the Securities Act of 1933 does not eliminate the requirement of state registration in those states in which no exemptions exist, or even insure that the offering will be acceptable to securities commissions of the various states in which the operator might wish to offer interests for sale."[1]

In that same paper, Mosburg indicates that:

"(1) In a few states, a *remedial* rather than preventive philosophy is adopted. In these states, one who has violated the fraud or other penal provisions of the local act is subject to criminal and/or civil liability. However, the investor is in fact protected only through his right to retribution, and to the extent that others are deterred from wrongful conduct by fear of retribution. . .

"(3) A final type of regulatory philosophy, adopted by a majority of states, requires that the proposed offering satisfy certain specified statutory standards. Under this qualification philosophy, the operator must satisfy the local commission that the offering meets applicable local tests, which vary from rather specific requirements to the 'fair, just and equitable' standards adopted by a number of jurisdictions."[2]

The most important point is that many states go beyond disclosure to regulation. If a program does not conform to certain standards, it cannot be sold in the state.

Appendix *C* contains a set of guidelines adopted by the North American Securities Administrators (NASA). NASA is an associa-

[1] Mosburg, Lewis G., Jr., "Mechanics of Registered and Unregistered Investor Drilling Programs," *Eighteenth Annual Institute on Oil and Gas Law and Taxation,* (Albany, N.Y.: Mathew Bender and Co., Inc., 1967) p. 142.

[2] Ibid., pp. 141, 142.

tion of state securities agencies. Those guidelines, while not binding upon the member states, do indicate what issues are of interest to state regulators.

While regulation of this kind is healthy, it can be costly and frustrating. It is not unusual for larger programs to sell in 30 to 40 or more states. Different states regard different things as important. What is acceptable in one state might not be acceptable in another.

A program manager must take into account the peculiarities of each state. Florida requires the sponsor to make a substantial investment in the program; California requires a suitability letter; Oregon requires escrowing of funds; Michigan wants commitments on the allocation of registration costs; Texas doesn't like installment sales; and New Hampshire apparently just doesn't like oil programs.

This variety of requirements means that extreme care must be exercised in structuring a program. Unfamiliarity with state requirements can lead to disaster. It is conceivable that a program could get through the SEC and fail to be admitted to a large number of states as it is described in the prospectus.

National Association of Securities Dealers (NASD)

The NASD is an organization whose membership includes a large portion of the securities dealers in this country. It has specific statutory authority to regulate, with SEC supervision, the business of dealing in securities. Traditionally, that regulatory authority has extended to such areas as selling practices, and sales materials.

Since almost all oil programs are sold by NASD members, the policies of the NASD are important. (It should be mentioned that some non-NASD sales organizations are regulated by a parallel SEC division). To the extent that the NASD follows its pattern of interest in sellers rather than issuers of securities, it would be reasonable to expect that its principal concern in oil programs would be suitability and selling materials.

While the NASD is certainly interested in suitability and sales materials, it has begun to take a more aggressive attitude toward the issuers of oil program interests. Its justification for this entry into the area of issuer regulation goes roughly as follows: The NASD is the responsible agency in assuring that selling practices are fair and reasonable. There are some oil program interests which, because of their management compensation, conflict of interest problems, or some other aspect of the program, are inherently loaded against the investor. In such cases, the selling agent, merely by selling the security is engaging in unfair and unreasonable sales practices. It follows that the NASD should establish certain standards to which an oil program must conform if it is to be sold by member firms.

This approach clearly amounts to an attempt to broaden the NASD's regulatory authority. Whether it will prevail remains to be seen. It is clear, however, that the NASD will continue to play an important role in the oil program industry. The only question is how large that role will ultimately be.

Oil Investment Institute (OII)

The OII is an association of oil programs. Formed in 1969, it was organized at a time when the industry was being threatened by regulation under the Investment Company Act of 1940. The SEC and the Congress had no industry spokesman to deal with and it was difficult for the government to distinguish between an industry point of view and the special pleading of particular companies.

Primarily because of the efforts of the Oil Investment Institute, the SEC agreed that regulation of oil programs under the Investment Company Act would be a mistake. From that point, the OII grew to 34 members. Although precise figures are not available, those members probably account for 50 to 60% of the sales in the industry.

The most significant achievement of the OII is the adoption of its Guide to Business Standards. (See Appendix *B*.) While those standards have no legal force, they do represent a good faith effort by the industry to set out standards of business practice which should be adhered to by any responsible management company.

The OII is only a trade association and in no way can it be said that it performs a regulatory function. It has, however, been very active in working with regulatory bodies. Members of the OII serve on the NASD's Oil and Gas Committee. The OII's Blue Sky Committee worked with the North American Securities Administrators in developing the Guidelines in Appendix *C*. The OII has worked continuously with the SEC since 1969 in an effort to provide more effective regulation.

The OII has shown itself to be genuinely concerned that new

effective regulation, going well beyond current law, be written and enforced at the federal level. Its Washington counsel, Mr. Manuel Cohen, is a former Chairman of the Securities and Exchange Commission and an extremely talented and effective attorney. Its special counsel, Mr. Lewis Mosburg, is an expert in the legal aspects of oil programs. Its general counsel, Mr. Donald Taylor, is an experienced oil program attorney who has made a great contribution to the OII. With this help, the organization has done an outstanding job of bringing together a group of strong competitors to protect investors from unethical program managers and to pursue the industry's legitimate interests.

Federal Legislation

In 1969, the United States Senate passed a bill intended to make amendments to the Investment Company Act of 1940. The 1940 Act is a regulatory statute that deals with mutual funds. One of the provisions of the amendments was that oil programs no longer would be excluded from regulation under the Act unless they met certain conditions. The most important conditions were that each participant be required to invest $10,000 or more during each 12-month period and that the program have no redemption or surrender rights.

The intent of the legislation was to regulate under existing law at least part of a growing industry that looked like a peculiar form of mutual fund. Since sales to unqualified investors and the weaknesses of redemption features were of particular concern to the government, it was those features that determined the exclusion.

While a few program managers felt that this approach would be acceptable, most were opposed. The following testimony is typical of the industry's response:

"1. Oil and gas programs are very unlike mutual funds, and their regulation under a law intended for mutual funds is inappropriate.

"2. The proposed amendment would damage the managers of oil and gas programs, their investors, and the independent petroleum industry in the United States. . .

"The passage of this amendment would certainly encourage oil managers to restructure their offerings in such a way as to avoid regulation.

"The practical effect of the amendment would be to abolish programs with less than a $10,000 minimum and a cash surrender value.

Very few programs would actually be regulated." [3]

Primarily because of the industry's response, the SEC changed its position. On December 11, 1969, Chairman Budge of the SEC told the House Subcommittee on Commerce and Finance:

"Prior to October of this year there was no organization representing this industry with whom we could discuss these matters and our staff was limited to holding discussions with such individual firms as presented themselves and were willing to consider the matter. There, however, now is such an organization, the Oil Investment Institute, which as I mentioned was created in October and which approached us subsequent to our appearance in November. Our staff has held discussions with them which have served to clarify the situation. They confirm our original view that there is a need for regulation to some degree of the type provided in the Investment Company Act for this industry. However, the industry vigorously opposes being regulated under the Investment Company Act. Such regulation would appear to present certain real problems for them, primarily because of the difficulty of accommodating the industry structure contemplated by the Investment Company Act with the structure in fact adopted by this industry in order to provide favorable treatment for its investors under the Internal Revenue Code.

"The tentative understanding reached between our staff and representatives of the Oil Investment Institute was that we could arrive at a mutually satisfactory solution by sitting down with them and drafting a regulatory statute which would provide certain safeguards for investors which they recognize may well be needed and which in some instances parallel provisions of the Investment Company Act but are especially tailored to the practices, problems, and operating methods of this industry." [4]

With this testimony in the record, it is clear that federal regulation of oil programs is going to occur. The industry, and primarily the OII, has been working with the SEC to come up with a satisfactory plan. By the mid-1970's, oil programs will be regulated by the federal government. If that regulation is intelligently drawn and applied by people who understand the business, it can transform the oil program industry into the dominant element in domestic petroleum exploration.

[3] Anderson, Truman E., Sr., Hearings Before the SubCommittee on Commerce and Finance of the Committee on Interstate and Foreign Commerce, House of Representatives, 91st Congress, First Session on H. R. 11995, S 2224, H. R. 13754, and H. R. 14737, Serial No. 91-34., pp. 733-734.

[4] *Ibid.*, p. 873.

APPENDICES

Appendix A

Members of the
Oil Investment
Institute

The Oil Investment Institute is an organization of oil program managers (see Chapter X). Formed in October, 1969, the OII has 34 members which account for about 50% to 60% of industry sales.

The OII Guide to Business Standards (Appendix B) was the first attempt by a responsible industry group to develop ethical and business standards for the oil program industry. Since adoption of the Standards in October of 1970, the OII has gained the respect of state and federal securities agencies and has become a very healthy influence in the industry.

General members of the OII are:

ADA OIL EXPLORATION CO.
6910 Fannin
Houston, Texas 77025

AMAREX, INC.
2000 Classen Center - Suite 614E
Oklahoma City, Oklahoma 73106

APACHE CORP.
1700 Foshay Tower
Minneapolis, Minnesota

BALLARD & CORDELL CORP.
230 Peachtree Street, N.W., Suite 1608
Atlanta, Georgia 30303

BASIN FUNDS, INC.
845 First National Building
Oklahoma City, Oklahoma 73102

BELCO PETROLEUM CORP.
630 Third Avenue
New York, New York 10017

CAMBRIDGE ROYALTY CO.
2600 Tenneco Building
Houston, Texas 77002

CANADIAN-AMERICAN
  RESOURCES FUND, INC.
2200 Continental National Bank Bldg.
Fort Worth, Texas 76102

CAYMAN MANAGEMENT CORP.
27608 Silver Spur Road
Palos Verdes Peninsula,
  California 90274

CLEARY PETROLEUM CORP.
310 Kermac Building
Oklahoma City, Oklahoma 73102

ENERGY PROGRAMS, INC.
122 East 42nd Street
New York, New York 10017

FERGUSON OIL COMPANY, INC.
100 Park Avenue Bldg., Room 1115
Oklahoma City, Oklahoma 73102

HANOVER PLANNING CO., INC.
8 Hanover Street
New York, New York 10004

ROY M. HUFFINGTON, INC.
2210 Tenneco Building
Houston, Texas 77002

HUSKY OIL LTD.
815 6th Street, S.W.
Calgary 2, Alberta, Canada

INEXCO OIL CO.
1200 Houston Club Building
Houston, Texas 77002

JOHNSTON PETROLEUM CORP.
Continental Oil Building
Denver, Colorado 80202

KANATA-OFFSHORE, INC.
1300 V&J Tower
Midland, Texas 79701

MAJOR, GIEBEL & FORSTER
1126 Vaughn Building
Midland, Texas 79701

MAY EXPLORATION
  VENTURES, INC.
1435 Republic National Bank
Dallas, Texas 75201

MAGNESS DRILLING
  FUND, LTD.
3535 N.W. 58th Street
Oklahoma City, Oklahoma 73112

McCULLOCH OIL CORP.
6151 West Century Blvd.
Los Angeles, California 90045

IDS OIL PROGRAMS
6151 West Century Blvd.
Los Angeles, California 90045

PATRICK OIL AND GAS CORP.
Box 747 - 744 W. Michigan Avenue
Jackson, Michigan 49204

PETRO-LEWIS CORP.
1224 Denver Club Building
Denver, Colorado 80202

PETRO-SEARCH, INC.
825 Petroleum Club Building
Denver, Colorado 80202

PRESIDIO OIL FUNDS, INC.
1900 Avenue of the Stars, Suite 1945
Los Angeles, California 90045

PRUDENTIAL FUNDS, INC.
1 New York Plaza
New York, N.Y. 10004

SENTINEL RESOURCES CORP.
600 Madison Avenue
New York, N.Y. 10022

SERIO EXPLORATION CO.
311 Market Street
Natchez, Mississippi 39120

SOUTHEASTERN
  EXPLORATION CO.
P.O. Box 44
Winter Park, Florida 32789

C & K PETROLEUM, INC.
611 First National Bank Bldg.
Houston, Texas 77002

TESORO PETROLEUM CORP.
8520 Crownhill
San Antonio, Texas 78209

WHITE SHIELD OIL &
  GAS CORP.
1601 South Main Street
Tulsa, Oklahoma 74101

Appendix B

**Statement of
Professional
Responsibilities and
Guide to Business
Standards and
Compliance Guidelines
for Members of
the Oil Investment
Institute**

INDEX

FOREWORD

BUSINESS STANDARDS AND COMPLIANCE GUIDELINES

     I.   Definitions
    II.   General Standards
   III.   Suitability Standards
   IV.   Conflict of Interest Standards
    V.   Disclosure Standards
   VI.   Compensation and Participation in Costs and Revenues
  VII.   Administration and Enforcement

115

FOREWORD

Because of the complex operating and financial characteristics inherent in oil and gas exploration, and the forms of legal organization required for direct participation by individual investors, managers of oil programs assume unique responsibilities. An oil program management company, by virtue of managing its investors' participation in oil and gas exploration, has additional responsibilities to its investors and to the public it serves. These additional responsibilities comprise the basis for certain fundamental standards by which a company seeking to serve as the manager of an oil program should conduct its business. The standards hereinafter set forth are those considered to be unique to oil program management, without reiterating ordinary responsibilities of business organizations.

Each member of the Oil Investment Institute ("OII") is deemed to assume responsibility, and shall be held accountable, for compliance with the Business Standards hereinafter set forth with respect to the creation and operation of any oil program if either (a) it is the Management Company of such program or (b) the Management Company of the program is directly or indirectly under its control.

Each Member Company of the OII is responsible to the participating investor for compliance with these standards. The member company may discharge its responsibilities either through its own employees (or those of a Management Company under its control) or by subcontract with others. Wherever appropriate, the language of these standards is to be interpreted to permit the member company to conduct its business in either manner. In all cases, however, the member company, and not the subcontractor, remains responsible to the participating investor for the satisfaction of the standards.

These standards were adopted by the Membership of the Oil Investment Institute on October 16, 1970, following a cooperative effort undertaken with the Professional Standards Committee for Petroleum Exploration Management Companies.

BUSINESS STANDARDS AND COMPLIANCE GUIDELINES

I. DEFINITIONS:

1. *Oil Program* — Any general or limited partnership, joint venture or similar organization which issues to investors, in a public offering, participating interests in petroleum exploration, development or production activities for the purpose of creating value for those investors and making available to them directly the tax incentives provided to the petroleum industry.

2. *Management Company* — The person directly responsible to investors in an oil program for the management of their invested capital.

3. *Affiliate* — Any person directly or indirectly controlling, controlled by

or under common control with the Management Company, or in which the Management Company or any officer or director thereof has a substantial financial interest.

4. *Conflict of Interest Situation* — Any situation which presents a reasonable possibility that a Management Company could act in a manner advantageous to itself or an affiliate at the expense or disadvantage of oil program investors.

5. *Person* — Any individual, or any corporation, partnership, joint venture or other entity.

6. *Qualified Petroleum Engineer* — A petroleum engineer whose competence and professional standing in matters of evaluation of oil and gas properties and petroleum reserves are generally recognized by banks and other financial institutions. It shall be the responsibility of the Executive Director of the OII, acting upon the advice and guidance of the Business Standards Committee, to maintain a list of such persons at the principal office of the OII and to provide the same to interested persons upon request.

7. *Member Company* — Any general member, or probationary general member, of the OII.

II. GENERAL STANDARDS

The nature of participation in petroleum exploration, development and production activities requires that individual investors rely completely upon the integrity and judgment of the Management Company, its officers and directors, and all persons directly or indirectly controlling the Management Company. Accordingly, in organizing and conducting oil programs, and in all dealings with or on behalf of program investors, Management Companies shall observe the highest standards of commercial honor, and shall respect the trust and confidence of program investors.

In addition to the specific standards hereinafter set forth, each Management Company shall:

1. Recognize and unfailingly honor an obligation, in conducting the affairs of an oil program, to deal fairly and reasonably with program investors at all times.

2. Exercise its best efforts on behalf of program investors; provide at all times adequate management personnel (including technical and administrative personnel) and related facilities, either through its own fulltime staff or on a contract basis, for the conduct of program activities in accordance with the description thereof in the prospectus; and undertake only such exploration and development activities as its facilities and personnel are reasonably capable of handling.

117

3. Possess adequate capitalization and liquidity to ensure the continued operation of the program in accordance with the description thereof in the prospectus, the safety of funds entrusted to its management by program investors and its ability to carry out any redemption feature incorporated in the program; at a minimum, the Management Company shall have a net equity at least equal to the minimum required of a corporate general partner in a limited partnership under existing rules and policies of the Internal Revenue Service, whether or not the program is organized as a limited partnership.

4. Conduct all program activities in accordance with a standard of prudence which a reasonable man would apply in investing his own funds for the objectives described in the prospectus for program activities, and, in particular, engage in debt financing of exploration activities only to the extent reasonably necessary and in the best interests of program investors.

5. Make use of tax incentives associated with petroleum exploration and development in a manner consistent with the Congressional intent in providing such incentives.

6. Comply fully with all laws applicable to the creation and operation of the program, including state and federal securities laws, all rules and regulations thereunder, and all requirements of pertinent self-regulatory authorities, as well as with these Business Standards.

III. SUITABILITY GUIDELINES

Petroleum exploration and development programs involve risk of loss to public investors and are, therefore, ordinarily suitable only for those investors who are in a financial position to accept this risk.

1. Interests in oil programs are ordinarily an appropriate form of investment only for persons with substantial other financial resources and annual income taxable in the higher income tax brackets. In general, therefore, interests in an oil program are deemed to be suitable for the investors to whom they are offered if, but only if:

A) Each investor is required to make a minimum payment to the program of at least $5,000 (in one sum or in installments) during the first twelve (12) months of the program's existence.

B) Each investor is required to supply written confirmation that:

1) He has a net worth of at least $200,000; or

2) Expects to have annual income of which some portion (not taking into account any deductions to be realized through participation in the program) is subject to income taxation at a federal rate of not less than 40% or an aggregate of city, state, and federal taxes of not less than 50%; and

3) That the investment is to be made solely for the personal account of the subscriber (or, in the case of a natural person, his spouse) and that the subscriber has no present agreement, understanding or arrangement to subdivide the interests subscribed for or to sell any portion of it to any other person.

2. It is recognized that, even though the above criteria are met, an investment in an oil drilling program may not be suitable for a particular investor. Fulfilling the above requirements shall not dispense with, nor act as a substitute for, the independent duty of the person selling or recommending the purchase of a participation to determine that the recommendation is suitable for such investor on the basis of information furnished by such customer after reasonable inquiry concerning the customer's investment objectives, financial situation and needs and any other information known by such person selling the interest.

3. It is recognized that variations in the anticipated tax consequences to investors, the nature and degree of the risks attending proposed program activities, and other factors, may warrant the employment of somewhat different standards and procedures to assure the suitability of interests. From time to time, on application by interested persons or on its own initiative, the Business Standards Committee will formulate and recommend to the Board of Governors the publication of special rules governing the obligations of Management Companies under this Article III in connection with particular programs or types of programs. In addition, the Business Standards Committee will from time to time review the general rules contained in paragraph 1 of this Article III, in the light of changes in the federal income tax laws and other pertinent considerations, and will recommend to the Board of Governors such modifications thereof as it may deem appropriate.

IV. CONFLICT OF INTEREST STANDARDS

The exercise of objective judgment in the best interests of program investors is made more difficult in situations where the interest of a Management Company or its affiliates may conflict with that of the investors. It is recognized, however, that the mere existence of certain conflict of interest situations may not necessarily be inconsistent with the best interests of program investors, provided that full disclosure is made to investors and adequate safeguards are observed. Management Companies shall observe the following rules with respect to all conflict of interest situations:

1. Before permitting any conflict of interest situation to exist in the creation or operation of an oil program, the Management Company shall fully disclose to program investors: (a) the nature of the conflict of interest;

and (b) the policies and procedures to be followed to insure that over-reaching or other unfairness to investors does not result.

2. Where a Management Company or its affiliate sells or otherwise provides property or services to, or obtains property from, an oil program under its management, the Management Company (and any member company by which it is controlled) assumes a heavy burden to assure that the terms of such transactions are fair and reasonable to program investors. In no event shall property or services (other than managerial or supervisory services to be rendered by the Management Company, the compensation for which, or the method for its computation, is fully disclosed in the prospectus) be sold or otherwise provided to, or acquired from, an oil program by the Management Company or any affiliate thereof, except in accordance with the following guidelines:

A. Property shall ordinarily be transferred to or acquired from a program at its cost, unless the Management Company has reason to believe that the cost of the property is either materially in excess of or materially lower than its fair value. The term "cost" for purposes of this subparagraph includes reasonable provision for interest, and service and carrying charges. Where property is transferred or acquired at a price other than cost, the Management Company shall take into account the opinion of a qualified independent petroleum engineer or other qualified independent expert as to its fair value.

B. Services shall be provided at their fair value, which shall in no event exceed the amount customarily charged for similar services where no affiliation exists between the person providing the services and the recipient thereof.

In any transaction described in this paragraph 2 in which property is transferred or acquired, or services are provided, at fair value, the Management Company shall create and maintain during the entire life of the program, and make available upon request by any program investor, a full written record of the basis for its determination of such fair value.

3. There may in the future come to the attention of the Business Standards Committee certain types of conflict of interest situations, or practices in connection therewith, which warrant absolute prohibition. Specific instances of such situations and practices will be set forth from time to time in interpretations of these Business Standards to be published by the Board of Governors on the recommendation of the Business Standards Committee. It shall in any event be deemed a violation of these Business Standards for any Management Company to:

A. Assign property to the program in which the Management Company retains mineral rights to adjacent acreage which the Management Company intends to explore or develop for its own account.

B. Permit program funds or other assets to be made available to the Management Company or any affiliate thereof for any purpose not related to the objectives of the program.

C. Reserve the right to divide expenditures, revenues, or assets of the program in any manner inconsistent with generally accepted accounting principles, and which might adversely affect the interests of program investors.

D. Deliberately undertake or continue program activities from which it expects to receive a profit, but from which there is no reasonable possibility of profit to program investors.

V. DISCLOSURE AND REPORTING STANDARDS

Full and complete disclosure is an extremely important element in investor protection. Disclosure takes three forms: (1) the prospectus contained in the registration statement which is on file with the Securities and Exchange Commission; (2) sales materials (any written materials provided to or made available for the use of potential program investors, other than the prospectus); and (3) reporting to investors.

1. It shall be deemed a violation of these Business Standards for a Management Company, directly or indirectly, to publish, circulate or distribute any prospectus, sales material or report to investors, or make any verbal communication to a potential investor, which it knows or has reason to know contains any untrue statement of material fact or is otherwise false or misleading.

2. At a minimum, the following guidelines should be followed for prospectuses filed with the Securities and Exchange Commission:

A. The disclosure requirements of the Securities and Exchange Commission should be fully complied with. Any additional disclosures required by state or local law, and self-regulatory agencies having jurisdiction, should also be met.

B. No matter what these agencies specify, adequate disclosure would include (to the extent permitted by federal and state securities laws, and rules and regulations thereunder):

(1) Full disclosure concerning all conflict of interest situations which are intended or reasonably anticipated to be created or allowed to exist in the formation or operation of the program;

(2) A clear indication of whether or not the Management Company or any affiliate thereof is an oil and gas operating company with its own technical staff; and the consequences of this for program in-

vestors, including a disclosure of any material compensation to be paid to third parties as a result of the absence of such a full technical staff;

(3) A clear statement of the total compensation and share of program revenues to be received by the Management Company and its affiliates, and a clear statement of the estimated percentage of the investors' dollars which will be used for the direct costs of acquiring, exploring and developing lease acreage and petroleum reserves, and the percentage of production revenues so developed which investors will receive therefor.

(4) Adherence to a standard set of accounts (as established by the Statistics and Terminology Committee) so that general cost categories between programs can be compared on an equivalent basis;

(5) Adherence to a standard set of definitions (as established by the Statistics and Terminology Committee) of commonly used terms in the oil program industry;

(6) A clear statement of the investment objectives of the program;

(7) Disclosure of the potential personal liability of the investor in respect of program activities, with due regard to the intended form of organization of the program, the responsibilities assumed by the Management Company, its financial strength, and the liability insurance to be maintained; and

(8) Disclosure of the material historical record of financial results from investor participation in past oil programs managed by the Management Company and its affiliates (including tax consequences to investors), and revenues received by the Management Company and its affiliates from such prior programs (including any profits from transactions of the type described in Article IV, paragraph 2).

3. In addition to any disclosures contained in the prospectus, the total package of sales materials provided to a potential investor in an oil program shall meet the following guidelines:

A. A balanced discussion of the offering should be presented, setting forth the risks, potential rewards, and advantages and disadvantages of the program, in straightforward, descriptive language.

B. Sales materials should explain that oil program investing is for high income individuals who have sufficient other resources to undertake the risks.

C. The compensation to the Management Company should be clearly and fully described, preferably in tabular form.

D. Any tax tables used should be carefully explained, and should include comparisons at the minimum tax bracket used in the determination of suitability.

E. There should be full compliance with any state or federal regulation and the requirements of appropriate self-regulatory bodies.

F. Each member of the OII should indicate in all sales materials that it is a member of the OII.

4. A copy of each preliminary and final prospectus covering an oil program, and any amendment thereto, shall be mailed to the principal office of the OII not later than the time such prospectus or amended prospectus is filed with the Securities and Exchange Commission. A copy of each item of sales materials shall be mailed to the principal office of the OII not later than the time such item is filed with the appropriate regulatory body or the time it is made available to potential program investors, whichever occurs first. The Grievance Committee, with the advice and approval of the Board of Governors, shall establish and carry out procedures for reviewing all such materials and notifying member companies of possible violations.

5. Because of the unique characteristics of oil programs, frequent and informative correspondence with oil program investors is particularly important. The following standards in investor communication should be observed as a minimum:

A. Reports should be made at least quarterly during any period in which material operations are being conducted. Annual financial statements for the oil program certified by independent public accountants shall be made available to program investors.

B. Each Management Company shall provide annually to investors in an oil program under its management financial statements of the Management Company (and affiliates, if pertinent) showing in reasonable detail, and in accordance with standards and procedures to be established by the Board of Governors upon the recommendation of the Statistics and Terminology Committee: (1) all revenues received by it and its affiliates from the program (not including its share of income, if any, by virtue of a capital contribution made on terms identical to those pertaining to investments by program investors), (2) all costs fairly attributable to its and its affiliates' provision of services and facilities to the program; and (3) all profits realized by it and its affiliates from transactions with the program of the type described in Article IV, paragraph 2.

C. Reports to investors should not be employed as sales materials unless accompanied by a current prospectus meeting all applicable requirements of law (including rules and regulations of the Securities and Exchange Commission and pertinent self-regulatory agencies) and of these Business Standards, and filed in accordance with paragraph 4 of this Article V.

D. To the extent permitted by law and pertinent regulatory authorities, each program should periodically provide its investors with value information in a standardized manner, in accordance with guidelines to be published by the Board of Governors upon the recommendation of the

Statistics and Terminology Committee. Such information, based upon engineering reports prepared by a qualified independent petroleum engineer, shall be provided to each investor in an oil program within 90 days after the close of the second full calendar year of the program's existence, as of the close of such year, and promptly after any material change in the information so provided.

E. Cash surrender values, redemption values and the like, insofar as they relate to petroleum reserves, should be based upon evaluation by a qualified independent petroleum engineer. In no event shall investor interests in a drilling program which have been redeemed or otherwise reacquired be sold or contributed by the Management Company to any other drilling program under its management or that of an affiliate.

VI. COMPENSATION AND PARTICIPATION IN COSTS AND REVENUES

1. The compensation received by the Management Company and its affiliates for the creation and operation of the oil program, including its share of revenues from program activities and the charges paid to it for the furnishing of materials, facilities, or services, must, in the aggregate, and in whatever form received, be fair and reasonable. Such compensation must be fully and understandably set forth in the prospectus and sales material, as provided in Article V of these Business Standards.

2. The compensation to be received by the Management Company must take into account:

A. The extent of services furnished by the Management Company; and

B. The extent to which the Management Company provides capital and participates in the costs and risks of the program.

3. In passing upon the reasonableness of the division of revenues derived from the conduct of program operations:

A. Management Companies bearing no portion of the expenses associated with obtaining production, and Management Companies which furnish no services other than the raising of capital and the providing of administrative and managerial services, shall be presumed to be entitled to receive only a minimum fraction of the revenues derived from program operations, generally not to exceed 10% of such program revenues, or the equivalent thereof.

B. Management Companies furnishing administrative, managerial, and technical services, including the furnishing of land, geological, engineering, and accounting personnel, and which, while bearing little or none of the costs associated with obtaining production, subordinate their interest in well revenues until payout to the investor of his share of the costs of such well, are presumed to be entitled to earn an intermediate fraction of program revenues, generally not to exceed 33⅓ % of the revenues from such well, or the equivalent thereof.

C. Management Companies furnishing administrative, managerial, and technical services, and which bear a portion of the costs associated with obtaining production, whether as a portion of total costs, or as all or a portion of specified expenditures, shall be presumed to be entitled to earn a higher fraction of initial well revenues, which generally shall not exceed the fraction of well and related lease costs, and the like, borne by it plus an additional 15% of the revenues from the related well, or the equivalent thereof.

D. The Business Standards Committee shall, with the approval of the Board of Governors, prescribe similar guidelines governing the reasonableness of the share of revenues being received by Management Companies whose cost and revenue formulas do not specifically fall within the examples set forth above.

VII. ADMINISTRATION AND ENFORCEMENT

1. The Grievance Committee will study and process complaints from investors, dealers or competitors to determine whether any alleged violation of this Guide to Business Standards has occurred, and may investigate possible violations on its own initiative. The Grievance Committee shall likewise, at the earliest practical date, furnish recommendations to the Board of Governors regarding an appropriate method of monitoring on an ongoing basis the activities and affairs of each member company to insure uniform compliance with these Business Standards.

2. The Business Standards Committee will from time to time, on its own initiative or upon receipt of requests for advice from member companies or other interested persons, recommend to the Board of Governors the publication of such interpretations of these Business Standards as it may deem appropriate.

3. The Grievance Committee may at any time, for the sole purpose of enforcing and administering these Business Standards, designate a national independent certified public accounting firm to request financial or other information from, or inspect the books, accounts and other records of, any member company. Within 10 business days after it is notified of the designation of an accounting firm for this purpose, the member company affected, if it objects to the firm so designated, may appoint one arbitrator by notice in writing given to the Executive Director; the Grievance Committee shall thereupon appoint a second arbitrator, and the two so chosen shall select a third. The three arbitrators shall then proceed, as promptly as possible, to designate the national independent certified public accounting firm which is to obtain the information or make the inspection desired by the Grievance Committee.

After obtaining the information or making the inspection authorized by the Grievance Committee, the firm so designated shall report to the Grievance Committee so much of the information thus acquired as shall in its opinion be relevant to the enforcement and administration of these Business Standards. It shall be a violation of these Business Standards for any member company to decline or refuse any such request for information or inspection; provided, however, that the recipient of the request may, within 10 business days after notification of the initial designation by the Grievance Committee of an accounting firm, apply to the Board of Governors in writing for modification or withdrawal of the request; in the event of such application, the recipient of the request shall be under no obligation to comply therewith until it has been formally notified of the decision of the Board of Governors with respect to the application, or the final designation of an accounting firm, whichever is later. To the fullest extent possible, all information obtained from any member company pursuant to this paragraph shall be maintained in the strictest confidence, and no person connected with the OII or any member company shall obtain, employ or divulge any such information for any purpose not directly related to the enforcement and administration of these Business Standards as provided in this Article VII.

4. The Grievance Committee shall make recommendations to the Board of Governors regarding appropriate sanctions to be imposed on, or other action with respect to, any member company which it finds, after due investigation and after affording the affected member an opportunity to respond to any charges proposed to be brought against it, to have violated these Business Standards. On the recommendation of the Grievance Committee, the Board of Governors by an affirmative vote of a majority of all members may impose any of the following sanctions for violation of these Business Standards: censure; suspension from membership for up to one year; or a fine of not more than $10,000. For repeated or especially serious violations, the Board of Governors may by an affirmative vote of two-thirds of all members expel any member company from the OII. In any case where disciplinary action is recommended by the Grievance Committee, the Board of Governors shall not be limited to imposing the sanction or sanctions recommended by the Grievance Committee, but may take any action in accordance with the foregoing which it deems appropriate. The Board of Governors shall promptly notify the Securities and Exchange Commission, the National Association of Securities Dealers and other appropriate regulatory authorities of any disciplinary action taken with respect to a member company. In addition, such action shall for a period of three years from the date thereof (or longer, if so decided by the Board of Governors), be disclosed in any prospectus filed with the Securities and Exchange Commission relating to a program of which the affected member is the Management Company or an affiliate thereof.

5. The Board of Governors will attempt to work out an understanding with the appropriate authorities for endorsement of these Business Standards, and the establishment of appropriate arrangements for their enforcement.
6. These Business Standards shall become effective on the tenth business day following their adoption, except to the extent that compliance with any provision hereof may conflict with applicable law or with contractual obligations assumed in good faith prior to that date. Any member for which immediate compliance with any provision hereof would be impractical or unduly burdensome may, on or before the effective date, submit a written application to the Grievance Committee for temporary relief from the provision or provisions in question, and shall be permitted to defer compliance therewith until such time as it has been notified of the decision of the Grievance Committee with respect to its application.
7. These Business Standards may be amended at any time by a two-thirds vote of the Board of Governors, in accordance with the procedures prescribed in the By-laws for their adoption.

Appendix C

**Guidelines for
Registration of
Oil and Gas
Offerings**

Introduction

The Guidelines for the Registration of Oil and Gas Offerings are a set of standards adopted by the North American Securities Administrators (NASA). NASA is a group of Securities Commissions in which each of the 50 states is represented.

Because of the increasing number and complexity of oil program filings, NASA asked its Committee on Oil and Gas Securities to submit a set of guidelines that could be used in each state in considering applications by oil program companies. That Committee, headed by Truman G. Holladay of Texas, held a number of meetings and generated the following guidelines.

GUIDELINES

I. DEFINITION OF TERMS

As used in the Guidelines, the following terms mean:

Administrative and Overhead Expenses — All costs and expenses of the sponsor made in connection with administering the program which are not directly allocable to a lease, well or prospect.

Affiliate — An affiliate of another person means (a) any person directly or indirectly owning, controlling, or holding with power to vote 5 per centum or more of the outstanding voting securities of such other person; (b) any person 5 per centum or more of whose outstanding voting securities are directly or indirectly owned, controlled, or held with power to vote, by such other person; (c) any person directly or indirectly controlling, controlled by, or under common control with such other person; (d) any officer, director, partner, co-partner or employee of such other person.

Development Well — A well drilled to a reservoir proven to be productive of oil or gas and expected to be extended to the drilling area.

Exploratory Well — Any other well.

Intangible Costs — Any costs generally accepted as current expense items for purposes of Federal Income Tax reporting.

Net Profit Interest — That interest in net operating income which becomes payable after recapture by the investor of all costs on a particular lease or drilling prospect.

Overriding Royalty Interest — A fractional undivided interest or right of participation in an oil and gas lease in the oil or gas, or in the proceeds from the sale of oil or gas, produced from a specific oil or gas property, such interest being free from the expense of development and operation of the property.

Participant — The purchaser of a unit in the oil and gas program.

Payout — That point at which the participant has received or credited to his account from the proceeds of production of oil and gas an amount, in dollars, equal to the cumulative, acquisition, exploration and development costs, rentals, production taxes, administrative and overhead expenses, lifting costs, and other costs of operation incurred by the sponsor attributable to or charged against the participant's interest.

Program — The total activities in which the proceeds of the offering and any additional proceeds generated thereby will be engaged.

Carried Interest — A working interest free or partially free of development costs.

Reversionary Interest — An interest with benefits defined by contract.

Royalty — An interest in production which is free from the expense of developing and operating the property to the owner.

Sponsor — The entity which originates and promotes an oil program.

Tangible Costs — Those costs which are generally accepted as capital expenditures for purposes of Federal Income Tax reporting.

Working Interest — The interest in a property which carries with it the obligation to pay a proportionate share of all costs during the period of time the working interest agreement is in effect including such costs as those resulting from exploration, development and operation of such properties.

II. THE PLAN OF BUSINESS

A. *Experience of Management*

Any enterprise with a sponsor without substantial experience and qualifications in the oil and gas industry either through its own staff or under tentative contract will be thoroughly scrutinized. If promotion of the sale of the offering appears to be the principal objective, the offering will be held contrary to the public interest.

B. *Capitalization of Sponsor and Investment by Sponsor*

1. The sponsor must be sufficiently capitalized to indicate his ability to perform the commitments which he makes in regard to the program. Audited balance sheet statements of the sponsors who are corporations

129

or partnerships with net equity less than the aggregate amount of securities being offered must appear in the prospectus, but in any case, audited balance sheets of all sponsors must be furnished with the registration statement.

2. Sponsor must meet the requirements of the Internal Revenue Service and have a favorable tax ruling assuring flow-through of tax benefits to the public investor or a favorable opinion of qualified tax counsel assuring flow-through tax benefits to the public investor.

3. (a) The sponsor must purchase a minimum of $100,000 in participation interests, net of commissions, in any entity which offers its oil and gas participation interests to the public. From this amount may be deducted 10% of the net equity of the sponsor; or

(b) The sponsor has the privilege of investing at least 10% of the amount paid, or to be paid, into the program by the participants.

C. *Interest of Sponsor*

Proceeds from the sale of units of the program being offered will not be used to prove up adjacent properties or properties in the geological prospect area belonging to sponsors or affiliates. Any exception to the foregoing rule must be fully disclosed in the prospectus and must be justified to the individual securities administrators.

D. *Compensation*

A maximum of 12½ % of the dollar amount of cash receipts to the program from a public offering is allowable to the program sponsor for organizational and offering expenses out of which must be paid any "management fees" for the first year of operation. Overhead and administrative expenses, fully audited, may be chargeable to the program and must be reasonable. If per well charges are made or contemplated, overhead and administrative charges must be reduced accordingly. Compensation to the sponsor (and its affiliates) of a program is limited as follows:

The participation in program revenues by the sponsor and any affiliate shall be reasonable, taking into account all relevant factors. Sponsors' retained interests may be considered reasonable if they meet the standards set forth in paragraphs (1) through (6) below. Any other combinations of fees, overriding royalty interests, and working or net profits interest, which are generally accepted as reasonable in the industry and are justified, in light of the entire offering, may be considered reasonable by the Commissioner:

1. Unless specifically provided for herein, overriding royalty interests and any other interests free of the burden of operating expenses will be looked upon with disfavor, as will be any form of compensation arrangement in which the sponsor or an affiliate engages in, or proposes to engage in, any activities which are unprofitable to the drilling program.

130

2. A 33⅓ % working interest or net profits interest in a lease, after payout, if there is no overriding royalty interest reserved by the sponsor.

3. A 1/16 overriding royalty interest, convertible after payout, not to exceed a 25% working interest or net profits interest in a lease.

4. A 1/16 overriding royalty interest plus not to exceed a 20% working interest or net profits interest, after payout, in a lease.

5. Under cost sharing arrangements by which the public investor bears all cost of exploration and the sponsor bears substantially all costs of development, a reversionary interest to the sponsor not in excess of 40% after payout may be deemed to be fair, and application of all revenue from development wells to accomplish payout of cost of development wells in such cases may be held to be reasonable; provided no money interest is charged to investors or to the program for the sponsor's funds committed to the program with respect to drilling costs in computing payouts.

6. In any other program in which a portion of the program costs are borne by the sponsor, an interest based upon the estimated percentage of drilling block or well costs, including costs of lease acquisition, to be borne by the sponsor, plus any additional interest deemed equitable in light of the entire offering may be permissible. Taking into account all relevant factors, a 50% interest in program revenues may be reasonable.

In no case may an overriding royalty interest of a sponsor and affiliates exceed 3/32, and royalty payments in any year for any lease may not exceed the net operating profits from the lease.

E. *Cash Redemption Values*

When cash redemption values of units are computed, such value must be clearly based on appraisal of properties by qualified independent petroleum engineers. Any evaluation by company personnel must be based on such independent appraisals.

F. *Periodic Reports*

No later than the end of the second year of the initiation of the program and at least annually thereafter, (or as value changes require) the sponsor shall provide each public investor with periodic reports which state the current value of his interest and progress of the enterprise arrived at by the use of procedures accepted by the industry. Annual audited financial reports and tax information shall be furnished to the investor in a form which may be used in the preparation of an investor's individual tax return. The report of value of the interest shall be based on an independent petroleum engineer's appraisal of the status of the properties.

G. *Future Exchanges and Automatic Reinvestment of Revenues*

1. Any future exchanges shall be made solely upon compliance with

131

applicable securities regulations, both federal and state.

2. *Automatic* reinvestment of revenues is considered unfair and contrary to the public interest. *Optional* reinvestment of revenues must follow complete information to the unit holder of the amount of revenue to which he is entitled as well as a full disclosure of the program into which his revenues will be reinvested at his election. The entity into which reinvestment is made must be registered with the appropriate minimums, as well as other standards, applicable to the entity as in a new program.

H. *Purchase of Producing Properties*

1. For drilling programs, purchase of producing properties in excess of ten per cent (10%) of the subscriptions to the program may be considered unreasonable and not in the interest of the public investor.

2. Oil and gas programs of the income type will be examined independently of these guidelines.

I. *Exculpatory Clause*

Sponsors and affiliates shall not be exonerated from liability to participants for any losses caused by gross negligence or by willful or wanton misconduct.

III. PLAN OF DISTRIBUTION

A. *Minimum Unit*

The minimum purchase of a program may not be less than $5,000 and the initial investment by a participant shall be no less than $5,000, all of which must be paid within 12 months from the date the program commences. Assignability of the unit must be limited so that no assignee (transferee) or assignor (transferor) may hold less than a $5,000 interest except by gifts or by operation of law.

B. *Assessment of the Unit*

If the unit may be assessed, a limitation must be placed upon the assessment. Dropout penalty for failure to pay an assessment must be fair to the public investor and clearly stated.

C. *Advertising Materials*

Sales of the units should be made by and through a prospectus. Supplementary materials must be submitted to the Commissioner in advance of use, and its use must either be preceded by or accompanied with an effective prospectus. Informational material may, and should be, distributed to unit holders on a periodic basis.

D. *Sale of Units*

1. Units of a program may be sold by sponsors and/or registered broker dealers and/or affiliates of sponsors. Officers and directors of sponsors who sell participation units must be licensed as broker dealers when required by statute and may be paid no commissions, either directly or indirectly, in any form in connection with the sale of the units.

2. Compensation to broker dealers shall be a cash commission. Indeterminate compensation to broker dealers, such as overriding interests and net profit interests, for example, is prohibited. In the absence of a firm underwriting, warrants or options to broker dealers are prohibited.

3. The broker-dealer, or the sponsor in the case of direct sales, shall take all action reasonably required to assure that program interests are sold only to purchasers for whom such interests are suitable.

Judgment of suitability of any particular program interest for an individual investor shall be based on the financial capacity of the purchaser, including the purchaser's net worth and income tax bracket, after a reasonable inquiry into the purchaser's financial condition and other related and relevant factors as may be appropriate.

The broker-dealer or sponsor shall retain all records necessary to substantiate the fact that program interests were sold only to purchasers for whom such securities were suitable. Securities Administrators may require broker-dealers or sponsors to obtain from the purchaser a letter justifying the suitability of such investment.

4. Compensation to wholesale dealers must be a cash commission, and such commission must be reasonable and fully disclosed.

5. Sales commissions based on assessment of units are prohibited.

IV. PROSPECTUS AND ITS CONTENTS

A. *Nature of the Organization*
The prospectus shall clearly state the nature of the business organization to be employed, e.g., joint venture, limited partnership, clearly stating the effect of the type of business organization on the individual investor, such as liabilities and rights to participate in the operation of the business. In the event that the offering is of a series of ventures, the prospectus must provide that no funds of one venture will be commingled with the funds of any other entity.

B. *History of Operations*
Sponsor's history of operations shall be fully disclosed, and when applicable, income from each program shall be scheduled.

C. *Area of Operations*
A general description of the areas in which it is anticipated that drilling operations will be conducted shall be set out.

D. *Maximum and Minimum*
The prospectus shall indicate the maximum amount of subscriptions to be sought from the public and the minimum amount of subscriptions necessary to activate the program. The minimum amount of funds to activate the program shall be sufficient to accomplish the objectives of the program, including "spreading the risk" and shall be set out in the prospectus. Any minimum less than $250,000 will be presumed to be inadequate to spread

the risk of the public investors. Provision must be made for the return to public investors of one hundred per cent (100%) of paid subscriptions in the event that the established minimum to activate the program is not reached.

E. *Tabular Representation of Interests*

The prospectus shall contain a tabular representation of interests of the parties to the venture, indicating the sharing of costs and expenses of the venture as well as the sharing in the distribution of the revenues of the venture. Where applicable, the table shall show interests before and after payout.

F. *Repurchase of Participations*

No representations shall be made that the program interests are readily marketable. If any provision is made for the repurchase of program interests, the program sponsor, or affiliate, shall be unconditionally obligated to repurchase a specified dollar amount of such interests each twelve month period in cash under a fully disclosed formula, which amount must be material. Valuation of the interests shall be determined by independent petroleum engineers annually on a specified date and interest holders may tender their interests for repurchase within 30 days following the valuation date. If the interests tendered exceed the maximum dollar amount which the sponsor or affiliate is obligated to repurchase in a twelve month period, those interests which are repurchased must be selected by lot.

G. *Conflict of Interest*

Prospectus must contain a section on conflict of interest, setting out the possible areas of conflict and the measures taken which protect the interest of the public investor in such instances.

Properties may be transferred from the sponsor or an affiliate to the program at cost to the sponsor or affiliate where this is done in all of the sponsor's programs without exception. Unless properties are always so transferred at cost, properties transferred to a program by a sponsor, which were acquired before the formation of the program, shall be sold at fair market value. If fair market value is materially greater than cost to the sponsor or affiliate, then fair market value must be established by qualified independent petroleum engineers. If the property is unproductive and/or unexplored, then the value shall be determined by a qualified independent expert. Any properties acquired by the sponsor or affiliate after formation of the program must be sold to the program at cost to the sponsor.

Any contracts, or other arrangements, for drilling or other services, or supplies furnished, to a program by the program sponsor or by a person or company affiliated with a program sponsor or a general partner must be at prices no higher than those normally charged in the same geographical areas by non-affiliated persons or companies dealing at arms-length. Such persons must be able to demonstrate that they are acting independently

134

and are engaging in a continuing business activity of providing drilling or other material services or supplies to the oil and gas industry. In the alternative such contracts or arrangements must follow open competitive bidding in which such affiliated persons or companies are the lowest responsible bidders.

Total gross income and any profits or losses, on an annual basis for the preceding three years, received by the program sponsor or persons or companies affiliated with the sponsor as a result of such contracts or arrangements must be disclosed in the prospectus.

H. *Use of Proceeds*

Prospectus must clearly account for the use of the proceeds of the offering. Proposed use should be set out in dollar amounts as well as percentages of the total offering proceeds.

I. *Completeness*

The prospectus must contain all material facts necessary for the public investor to make an investment decision and for the administrator to make a finding after examination.

Appendix D

Fee Structure
Analysis

Introduction

At about the time that the NASA Guidelines (Appendix C) were put into final form, the management of Petro-Search, Inc. was faced with a decision. In order to minimize blue-sky problems, the company wanted to have its compensation pattern clearly within the Guidelines. It also wanted to know, in detail, how much each of several compensation arrangements would cost the investor. With that information it would also be possible to construct a study which related finding costs to oil program "success."

Petro-Search, therefore, asked Mr. Richard Roda to prepare a study on the subject. That study is contained in full in this Appendix.

This kind of study has limitations. In Chapter VII, it was suggested that:

"Comparisons of incentive compensation arrangements can be misleading because of the need to make assumptions. The compensation figures must be used on a consistent set of values for finding, developing and producing oil. Those values must be assumed.

"The problem is that there is a wide variety of reasonable assumptions. Different incentive arrangements may appear more or less desirable—depending upon the assumptions."

Despite this warning, it is true that a study of compensation and finding costs can be instructive. It certainly has value for situations similar to the model. While its results cannot be regarded as precise answers, at least those results show the range in which programs function.

A summary letter

Petro-Search, Inc.
Mr. Truman E. Anderson
825 Petroleum Club Bldg.
Denver, Colorado 80202
Dear Sir:

In accordance with your request, an analysis has been made of seven various compensation structures common in the drilling program industry. All structures are acceptable to the Committee on Oil and Gas Interests of the North American Securities Administrators. The purpose of this study was two-fold: 1) to compare fee structure for varying degrees of success and, 2) attempt to find the maximum net finding cost per barrel net to the investor which can be supported and still have an economically "successful" program.

A base model consisting of two dry holes and a completed well was created. This model was then adjusted to yield a finding cost per equivalent barrel of $1.00, $1.33 and $2.00 respectively. The various Management Company compensation methods were then calculated for each finding-cost model.

Before interpreting results, a standard of "success" must be set. If "success" is defined as having the present worth of future reserves (discounted at some nominal rate—in this report eight percent per annum) just equal to the original investment, two interesting conclusions can be inferred:

1. The range of net finding costs to the investor is narrow. For all fee structures examined[1] the maximum base finding cost allowable for "success" is $1.60 per barrel and the minimum is $1.46 per barrel. Exhibit V in the main body of the report translates this $1.60 per barrel to the *investor net finding cost which has a maximum allowable value of about $2.10 per barrel* (depending on specific fee structure).

2. In the finding cost range of $1.30-$2.10 per barrel where most Sponsors might be expected to operate, results to the investor are not sensitive to the type of fee structure. In fact, at a base finding cost of $1.50 per barrel, the maximum range of present worth profit to the investor for all fees[1] is seven percent plus-or-minus.

Results are discussed in detail in the attached report.

Thank you for the opportunity to be of service.

Yours very truly,
R. H. Roda

RHR:ss
Enclosures

The Analysis

Fee structures in the Oil and Gas Drilling Program Industry are varied as the inventive ingenuity of the Sponsor permits. Not only are there a great many different methods of reimbursing the Management Company, but, profits

---

[1] With the exception of two cases. One, the base case in which no fees whatsoever are charged and two, a fee structure in which the Sponsor pays all tangible capital costs and receives 50% of production.

from any given fee structure are a function of the degree of success of that program. For example, an overriding royalty may be onerous to the investor in a program which will never payout. Yet in an extremely successful program the same overriding royalty to the Sponsor may result in a smaller share of revenue than other generally accepted fee structures. Thus, fee structures must not only be compared against each other but also for a varying degree of success.

This report examines profit to the investor under seven different fee structures all within the guidelines deemed acceptable by the Committee on Oil and Gas Interests of the North American Securities Administrators (NASA). Three simple models have been created based on a finding cost of $1.00, $1.33 and $2.00 per net barrel of reserves. These three base cases do not include any form of compensation to the Sponsor. They are intended to represent the base investment in drilling and, as such, are comparable to finding costs as generally discussed in the oil and gas industry. The fee structures are then added to each finding cost and compared.

Remuneration of a sponsor for its efforts is complex and depends on many variables. No attempt has been made herein to examine all possible considerations. Instead, a series of relatively simple economic models have been created and used for comparison purposes.

The basic model is discussed in detail in Exhibit 1. Briefly, it consists of two dry holes and one successful producer. The productive life varies between 21 and 25 years with some 64 percent of the total net operative revenue being received in the first six years. Both oil and natural gas are produced from the successful well. The productive life and the shape of the income stream plotted versus time are presumably similar to a "typical" or "average" industry well.

Reserves produced by the successful well are adjusted to yield the finding costs discussed above. Future capital requirements (in the sixth year of productive life) have been included. In all cases these costs come after any reversion of working interests.

Profitability to the investor has been calculated on the following bases:

1. A 3/32nd overriding royalty throughout life.

2. No overriding royalty interest but a 33-1/3rd percent working interest in a lease after payout.

3. A 1/16th overriding royalty interest convertible after payout of a lease to a 25% working interest.

4. A 1/16th overriding royalty interest throughout life plus a 20% working interest, after payout, in a lease.

5. A cost-sharing arrangement by which the intangible portion of exploration and development costs are borne by the participant and the Sponsor bears all initial tangible costs and receives a 50% interest in the program.

138

6. As above, except the Sponsor received a 30% interest in the program.

7. The Sponsor retains a 1/16th overriding royalty throughout life plus a 10% working interest, after payout, in a lease.

In all cases the required future development capital is shared on a basis of working interest in effect at the time of expenditure.

In cases 2, 3 and 4 above, the Sponsor has the option of either a working interest or a similar net profits interest. This study has assumed the working interest option in all cases. Dollar differences to the investor are slight. A net profits interest, however, would result in additional profits to the Sponsor.

Ten percent of the dollar amount of cash receipts to the program is taken by the Management Company for organizational and offering expenses. Overhead and administrative expenses are assumed to be equal for all cases and are included in operating expenses for purposes of calculation.

Exhibits 2, 3 and 4 summarize the results to the investor for each of the three base models. The arrangement of the fee structures across the Exhibits from left-to-right is in order of decreasing benefit to the investor. In other words, the third column is "better" for the investor than the fourth; the fourth is better than the fifth, etc.

"Better" for the purposes of this study has been defined as percent present value profit. There are several definitions of best in an economic sense. Some of these would be undiscounted profit, total future income, discounted future income, earning power and payout time. Obviously, present worth values are more meaningful than any of the undiscounted criteria. Of the remaining choices, percent present value profit has been chosen as the most valid ranking criteria.

A graphical summary of results is presented in Exhibit 5 where percent present worth profit to the investor is plotted for each fee structure against varying degrees of success (finding cost).

Several interesting conclusions can be inferred.

First, curves 6 and 7, in which the Sponsor pays all tangible capital costs and receives 50% and 30% of production are extreme cases. A 40% revenue sharing program would place this fee structure in the middle of the range covered by the remaining compensation methods.

Assuming the drilling program industry operates within a finding cost range from $1.30 to $2.00 per barrel the curves (within the specific limitations discussed above) show remarkably little spread.

In fact, the less successful the industry is, the closer the curves become. If the average base finding cost of a program is $2.00 per barrel an investor can see no difference between fee structures 2, 3, 4, 5, 7 and 8. Whatever the fee structure of the program in which he has invested, his present worth value is 72 cents per dollar invested (plus-or-minus 3 cents).

If "success" for a drilling program is defined as achieving a present worth for the investor of $1.00 per dollar invested, then, the maximum base finding

139

cost (not including Sponsors' fees) that can be supported is about $1.50 per barrel. This definition of "success" assumes some tax-reduction of the investors investment. For example, an investor in a 50% tax bracket who invests $1.00 and thus obtains a 70% tax deduction has a net (after tax) investment of 65¢. Achieving a present worth value of reserves of $1.00 would thus result in a profit of 35¢ or some 54% based on the *net* investment of 65¢.

No calculation of Federal Income Tax has been included in this analysis. Differences in tax deductibility in various fee structures have not been examined.

Exhibit 6 represents a cross-plot of data from Exhibits 2, 3 and 4 and shows the finding cost per barrel to the investor for a given Sponsors' cost. For example, if the Sponsor generates (or accepts) drilling ventures with a base (before fees or compensation) of $1.50 per barrel the investor would experience the following:

a) Under a compensation system under which the Sponsor receives a 3/32nd overriding royalty (curve 2) the investors effective cost is $1.86 per barrel.

b) Under a system under which the Sponsor takes a 33⅓% working interest after payout (curve 3) the investors effective cost is $2.21 per barrel.

Using the correlations between investor and Sponsors' finding cost, Exhibit 5 can be re-plotted against net investors finding cost per barrel. Exhibit 7 is such a plot and indicates, for each fee structure the maximum net finding cost the investor can sustain and yet have a "successful" investment. Note that, for all fee structures studied, the minimum acceptable cost ranges from $1.90 to $2.03 per barrel. The range is narrow and indicates the drilling program industry, as a whole and almost regardless of fee structure, has a minimum target of some $2.00 per barrel.

Exhibit 1
ECONOMIC MODEL

Discussion of Model

The basic model assumes three wells are drilled. Two are abandoned as dry holes and the third is completed as a gas well. Capital cost is as follows:

	Tangible	Intangible	Total
Dry Hole			
Leasehold Cost	0	$10,000	$ 10,000
Drilling Cost	0	80,000	80,000
Subtotal — dry hole	0	$90,000	$ 90,000
Producer			
Leasehold Cost	$10,000	0	$ 10,000
Drilling and Completion	70,000	$90,000	160,000
Subtotal — producer	$80,000	$90,000	$170,000

The model costs (two dry holes and one producer) will total $350,000 of which $80,000 or 23% is tangible capital costs. In addition a $15,000 future capital cost for the producing well is incurred after six years. Of this amount $10,000 is assumed to be tangible capital. All capital and leasehold costs on dry holes are assumed to be intangible costs.

The producing well is assumed to be burdened with a normal one-eighth landowner's royalty and an additional 5% overriding royalty (not to the Management Company).

Product prices are as follows:

Natural gas
   Initial gas price is 20¢/MCF and escalates 1¢/MCF each 5 years.

Condensate
   The price per barrel of $3.284 remains constant over life.

Natural gas is converted to equivalent barrels of oil at a ratio of 1642 MCF per barrel (based on product prices).

Production taxes on both oil and gas are 4% of gross. Initial production rate is held constant for 2 years, then declined exponentially until the economic limit is reached. Total (100%) working interest reserves for the three cases are:

Total Working Interest Reserves

Finding Cost/ Equivalent Bbl. Oil	Condensate (Bbls.)	Natural Gas MMCF	Total Equivalent Bbls.
$1.00	49,500	4,950	394,970
$1.33	37,125	3,712	263,000
$2.00	24,750	2,475	175,000

Tables I, II and III present, respectively, income and expense detail for the $1.00, $1.33 and $2.00 per barrel finding-cost cases. For these three base cases no Management Company fees of any kind are included.

EXHIBIT 2
BASE FINDING COST $1.00/BBL.

ECONOMIC ANALYSIS	Sponsor' Fees	No Fees Base Case (Total Profit Potential of Model)	Pays Tangible Capital Costs— Takes 30% Working Interest		3/32 ORRI	
			Investor	Sponsor	Investor	Sponsor
Capital Investment:						
Organizational &						
Offering Expenses		$ 0	$ 27,000	$ 0	$ 35,000	$ 0
Initial Capital		350,000	270,000	80,000	350,000	0
Subtotal—Cost Basis		350,000	297,000	80,000	385,000	0
Future Costs		$ 15,000	$ 10,500	$ 4,500	$ 15,000	$ 0
Net Reserves:						
Bbls.		49,501	34,651		43,876	
MMCF		4,950	3,465		4,387	
Finding Cost Per Equiv.						
Bbl. Reserves		$ 1.00	$ 1.21		$ 1.24	
Net Income:						
Undiscounted		$1,016,763	$711,734		$887,017	
Present Worth @ 8%		694,577	486,204		608,797	
Profit:						
Undiscounted						
Dollars		666,763	414,734		502,017	
Percent		191	140		130	
Present Worth @ 8%						
Dollars		334,751	189,204		223,797	
Percent		93	64		58	
Average Annual Earning						
Power:		33.0%	24.8%		23.4%	
Payout Time (years):		2.75	3.44		3.56	

1/16 ORRI Plus a 10% Working Interest After Payout		1/16 ORRI Convertible to a 25% Working Interest After Payout		1/16 ORRI Plus a 20% Working Interest After Payout		33⅓% Working Interest After Payout		Pays Tangible Capital Costs—Takes 50% Working Interest	
Investor	Sponsor	Investor	Sponsor	Investor	Sponsor	Investor	Sponsor	Investor	Sponsor
$ 35,000	$ 0	$ 35,000	$ 0	$ 35,000	$ 0	$ 35,000	$ 0	$ 27,000	$ 0
350,000	0	350,000	0	350,000	0	350,000	0	270,000	80,000
385,000	0	385,000	0	385,000	0	385,000	0	297,000	80,000
$ 13,500	$1,500	$ 11,250	$3,750	$ 12,000	$3,000	$ 10,000	$5,000	$ 7,500	$ 7,500
41,967		38,617		38,183		35,630		24,750	
4,197		3,862		3,818		3,563		2,475	
$ 1.29		$ 1.41		$ 1.42		$ 1.52		$ 1.69	
$854,239		$794,202		$778,213		$734,511		$508,381	
589,655		550,708		541,919		516,639		347,288	
469,239		409,202		393,213		349,511		211,381	
122		106		102		91		71	
204,655		165,708		156,919		131,619		50,288	
53		43		41		34		17	
22.5%		19.9%		19.4%		18.0%		12.3%	
3.63		3.90		3.95		4.13		5.34	

EXHIBIT 3
BASE FINDING COST $1.33/BBL.

	Base Case (Total Profit Potential of Model)	Tangible Take 30% Investor	Sponsor	3/32 ORRI Investor	Sponsor
Capital Investment:					
Organizational & Offering Expense	$ 0	$ 27,000		$ 35,000	
Initial Capital	350,000	270,000		350,000	
Subtotal—Cost Basis	$350,000	$297,000		$385,000	
Future Costs	15,000	10,500		15,000	
Net Reserves:					
Barrels	37,125	25,987		32,906	
MMCF	3,712	2,599		3,291	
Finding Cost Per Equiv.					
Bbl. Reserves	1.33	1.61		1.65	
Net Income:					
Undiscounted	$740,596	$511,697		$633,723	
Present Worth @ 8%	509,973	354,985		442,644	
Profit:					
Undiscounted					
Dollars	390,596	214,697		248,723	
Percent	112	72		65	
Present Worth @ 8%					
Dollars	159,973	57,985		57,644	
Percent	46	20		15	
Average Annual Earning					
Power:	20.1%	13.2%		12.0%	
Payout Time (years):	3.91	5.1		5.3	

144

	1/16 ORR Plus 10% WI After Payout		1/16 — 25%		1/16 Plus 20% APO		33⅓% WI		Tangible Takes 50%	
	Investor	Sponsor	Investor	Sponsor	Investor	Sponsor	Investor	Sponsor	Investor	Sponsor
	$ 35,000		$ 35,000		$ 35,000		$ 35,000		$ 27,000	
	350,000		350,000		350,000		350,000		270,000	
	$385,000		385,000		385,000		385,000		297,000	
	13,500		$ 11,250		$ 12,000		$ 10,000		$ 7,500	
	31,683		29,355		29,054		27,412		18,562	
	3,168		2,936		2,905		2,741		1,856	
	1.71		1.85		1.87		1.98		2.26	
	$616,533		579,729		566,918		543,999		365,498	
	433,504		409,567		402,872		390,868		253,561	
	231,533		194,729		181,918		158,999		68,498	
	60		51		47		41		23	
	48,504		24,567		17,872		5,868		(43,439)	
	13		6		5		2		(15)	
	11.5%		9.8%		9.3%		8.4%		4.2%	
	5.4		5.9		6.0		6.5		9.3	

EXHIBIT 4
BASE FINDING COST $2.00/BBL.

	Base Case (Total Profit Potential of Model)	Tangible Take 30%		3/32 ORR	
		Investor	Sponsor	Investor	Sponsor
Capital Investment:					
Organizational & Offering Expense	$ 0	$ 27,000	$ 0	$ 35,000	$ 0
Initial Capital	350,000	270,000	80,000	350,000	0
Subtotal—Cost Basis	$350,000	$297,000	$80,000	$385,000	$ 0
Future Costs	$ 15,000	$ 10,500	$ 4,500	$ 15,000	$ 0
Net Reserves:					
Barrels	24,751	17,326		21,938	
MMCF	2,475	1,732		2,194	
Finding Cost Per Equiv.					
Bbl. Reserves	2.00	2.42		2.48	
Net Income:					
Undiscounted	$445,228	$311,659		$380,429	
Present Worth @ 8%	319,695	223,786		276,516	
Profit:					
Undiscounted					
Dollars	$ 95,228	$ 14,659		$ (4,571)	
Percent	27	5		(1)	
Present Worth @ 8%					
Dollars	$(30,305)	$(73,214)		(108,485)	
Percent	(9)	(25)		(28)	
Average Annual Earning					
Power:	5.6	—		—	
Payout Time (years):	7.9	—		—	

1/16 ORR +10% WI APO		1/16 OR −25% APO		33⅓% WI APO		1/16 OR +20% WI APO		Tangible Take 50%	
Investor	Sponsor	Investor	Sponsor	Investor	Sponsor	Investor	Sponsor	Investor	Sponsor
$ 35,000	$ 0	$ 35,000	$ 0	$ 35,000	$ 0	$ 35,000	$ 0	$ 27,000	$ 0
350,000	0	350,000	0	350,000	0	350,000	0	270,000	80,000
$385,000	$ 0	$385,000	$ 0	$385,000	$ 0	$385,000	$ 0	$297,000	$80,000
$ 13,500	$ 1,500	$ 11,000	$ 3,750	$ 15,000	$ 0	$ 12,000	$ 3,000	$ 7,500	$ 7,500
21,414		20,120		19,235		19,953		12,375	
2,141		2,012		1,923		1,995		1,237	
2.54		2.70		2.82		2.72		3.38	
$378,826		$365,070		$353,486		$355,623		$222,613	
276,999		267,590		264,127		263,090		159,847	
$ (6,174)		$(19,930)		$(31,514)		$(29,377)		$(74,387)	
(2)		(5)		(8)		(8)		(25)	
(108,001)		$(117,410)		$(120,873)		$(121,910)		$(137,153)	
(28)		(30)		(31)		(32)		(46)	
—		—		—		—		—	
—		—		—		—		—	

Present worth profit vs. finding cost

Exhibit 5

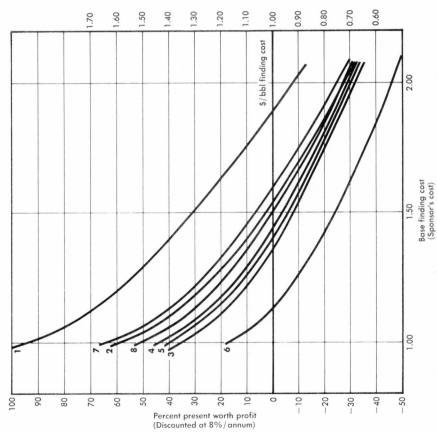

Legend

Curve No.	Sponsors' fee structure
1	Base case—no fees
2	3/32nd overriding royalty
3	33⅓% working interest (WI) after payout
4	1/16 overriding royalty convertible after payout to a 25% WI
5	1/16 overriding royalty _plus_ a 20% WI after payout
6	Pay all tangible costs and take a 50% WI
7	Same as No. 6 except take a 30% WI
8	1/16 overriding royalty _plus_ a 10% WI after payout

Present worth/$1.00 subscribed, dollars

$/bbl finding cost

Base finding cost
(Sponsor's cost)

Percent present worth profit
(Discounted at 8%/annum)

Base finding costs vs. investor costs

Exhibit 6
(No sponsor reimbursement)

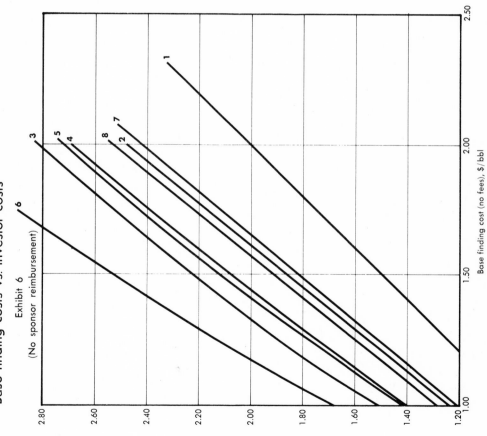

Legend		
Curve No.	**Sponsors' fee structure**	
1	Base case—no fees	
2	3/32nd overriding royalty	
3	33⅓% working interest (WI) after payout	
4	1/16 overriding royalty convertible after payout to a 25% WI	
5	1/16 overriding royalty *plus* a 20% WI after payout	
6	Pay all tangible costs and take a 50% WI	
7	Same as No. 6 except take a 30% WI	
8	1/16 overriding royalty *plus* a 10% WI after payout	

Investors' finding cost, $/bbl

Base finding cost (no fees), $/bbl

Present worth profit vs. investors' finding cost
Exhibit 7

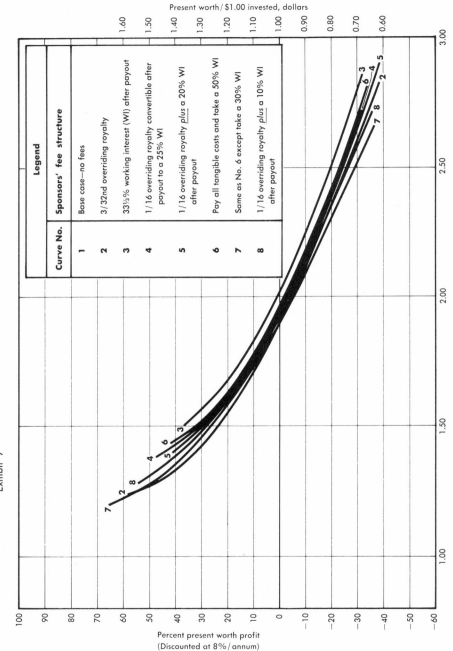

Present worth/$1.00 invested, dollars

| | 1.60 | 1.50 | 1.40 | 1.30 | 1.20 | 1.10 | 1.00 | 0.90 | 0.80 | 0.70 | 0.60 |

Legend

Curve No.	Sponsors' fee structure
1	Base case—no fees
2	3/32nd overriding royalty
3	33⅓% working interest (WI) after payout
4	1/16 overriding royalty convertible after payout to a 25% WI
5	1/16 overriding royalty *plus* a 20% WI after payout
6	Pay all tangible costs and take a 50% WI
7	Same as No. 6 except take a 30% WI
8	1/16 overriding royalty *plus* a 10% WI after payout

Investors' finding cost (after fees), $/bbl

Percent present worth profit
(Discounted at 8%/annum)

Appendix E

Introduction

While there is no such thing as a "typical" oil program, it may be useful to construct a hypothetical situation. By following the decision making process through the life cycle of an oil program, it should be possible to display how a typical oil program might work.

In order to make this hypothetical construct meaningful, it will be necessary to be quite specific. That specificity will exclude from discussion a broad range of possibilities which could occur. Nevertheless, enough issues are mentioned to give a general impression of the workings of an oil program.

HOW A TYPICAL OIL PROGRAM WORKS

I. *The Organizational Phase* — ABC Oil Company is an independent oil company headquartered in Houston, Tex. It has exploration offices in New Orleans, La., and Calgary, Alberta. In its 10 years of existence, ABC Oil has been successful in exploration for oil and gas in Texas and Louisiana. The Calgary office was added 2 years ago.

The company has always generated its exploration funds internally and by selling interests to a few very wealthy investors. In the last several years, however, two factors have added to the company's need to augment its exploration budget. First, several of its large private investors have died, and their estates have not continued to invest. Second, the Calgary office has great potential in the long run, but the commitment to acquire a strong land position means that there will be a negative cash flow for several years. At the same time, ABC Oil has noticed the growing success of oil programs.

A decision is made to form an oil program. A law firm is retained to help in writing a prospectus. In order to answer the questions raised by the S.E.C. in the registration statement, the following issues must be resolved:

151

1. *The dollar amount to be registered.*

It is decided that $5-million is the proper amount. The management of the company feels that $5-million can be prudently spent in a 1-year period through the company's three exploration teams in Houston ($2 million), New Orleans ($2 million), and Calgary ($1 million).

2. *The legal form:*

Counsel to ABC recommends that a limited partnership form be used. The principal reason is that a limited partnership form insulates investors against liability beyond the amount of their investment.

This decision means that ABC must restructure its corporate framework. A new company, ABC Oil Programs, Inc., is organized. The new company, a wholly-owned subsidiary of ABC Oil, will act as General Partner. ABC Oil capitalizes ABC Oil Programs, Inc. with $500,000. This substantial investment is made to ensure that the General Partner has adequate assets for the Internal Revenue Service. The IRS may argue that the partnership is taxable as a corporation unless certain tests are met. One of those tests is substance in the General Partner.

3. *Plan of distribution*

The management of ABC believes that it can persuade about a dozen NASD member firms to sell partnership interests. Meetings have been held with brokerage firms in Houston and New York. Two of those firms are particularly promising. They are impressed with the record of ABC Oil Company and feel that their sales forces could sell the partnership interests.

Neither of the firms has had much experience in selling oil program interests. Consequently, they are willing to sell ABC actively only if ABC provides wholesaling support.

For that reason, ABC Oil forms another subsidiary, ABC Securities, Inc. That company, an NASD member, is a brokerage firm whose job it is to promote the sale of ABC limited partnerships. Two men are hired away from competing oil programs. Their job is to go to the various offices of the securities firms interested in ABC Oil Programs. They train sales people, work with prospective investors, provide sales information and act as a link between the management of ABC Oil and its dealers.

4. *Application of Proceeds*

Since its inception, the company has been exploration oriented. While the company often is involved in lower risk prospects (because of the need to maintain a minimum cash flow level), its expertise is in exploration.

For that reason, it is not at all difficult to decide how partnership funds will be invested. Sixty percent of the proceeds (after sales costs and overhead charges) will be allocated to exploration. The remaining 40% will be used for development. The development budget can be expended on exploratory lands if exploration is successful. If it is not, the development budget will be used in lower risk areas to ensure that the program is not a total failure.

5. *Assessments*

While the management of ABC Oil feels that an assessment feature would be wise, it is persuaded not to have one by the wholesalers. The sales people feel very strongly that an assessment feature, even if restricted to a set amount, would be harmful to sales.

If the development budget is not adequate to finance all the development necessary, production loans will be used. These loans will defer the time at which income can be distributed to investors, but that disadvantage is judged to be overcome by the avoidance of an assessment feature.

6. *Timing and frequency of closing dates*

Although it may seem to be only a small issue, the sales group and the management group have their sharpest disagreement over the timing and frequency of partnership closing dates.

Management wants to have one partnership per year that closes in March or April. The reasoning is as follows:

a) Administrative costs will be reduced with one rather than multiple partnerships each year;

b) A closing early in the year maximizes the time available to reach writeoff objectives;

c) A closing early in the year gives the company more time to find the best available drilling prospects before the end of the tax year.

The sales people and the firms who want to sell ABC Oil Programs, argue:

a) One closing a year would be catastrophic. Of the $5 million registered, only $1 million might be sold. The reason is that it takes a great deal of effort to get a sales force involved in a program. One closing a year means that the sales people will lose interest between closings. Continuous interest can be retained only by having frequent closings;

b) While it may be ideal for the management to have its closings early in the year, the fact is that in April, most investors are worried about *last* year's taxes, not this year's. As an industry, oil programs have always raised more in the last 6 months of the year than in the first 6 months.

These very practical arguments are persuasive with the management. They agree to four partnerships per year—closing on April 1, July 1, October 1, and December 1.

7. *Compensation*

The possible methods of compensation to ABC Oil are varied. The format chosen is based on two important objectives:

a) A desire to invest ABC Oil's own funds in a manner which does not compete with investors;

b) A desire to maximize tax savings to investors in the initial year of the program.

These objectives imply that a tangible/intangible sharing arrangement should be used (see Chapter VII for a description of this approach). Given that decision, however, what specifics are to be employed? The following issues must be resolved:

a) Should the manager take a fixed percentage of revenues or should he take a pro rata share of each well that is determined by his actual investment in tangibles? If he takes a fixed percentage (perhaps 40%), his actual contribution of tangible cost may be higher than expected (and hurt the manager) or lower than expected (and hurt the investor). On the other hand, if he takes a pro rata share, won't he have a strong incentive to make "Cadillac completions" on good wells? He could increase his share simply by spending as much as he can on producers after investors have taken the dry hole risk;

b) Investment by ABC Oil in tangibles only will increase its tax liability by making it capitalize amounts which in former years it had expended;

c) The Calgary office feels that a tangible/intangible sharing arrangement is inappropriate for Canadian operations. Canadian exploration requires large investments in mineral rights. The cost of those mineral rights must be capitalized;

d) There is a conflict of interest problem in deciding to complete or not to complete for production on "marginal" wells. Suppose, for example, that $100,000 has been invested to get a well down to its objective depth. Also suppose that the manager gets 40% of the property for paying all tangible costs. The well is estimated to have $150,000 in recoverable reserves. It costs $75,000 in tangible expenditures to complete the well. This implies that:

1.) For a $75,000 investment, the manager will get $60,000;

2.) For no additional investment, the investors will get $90,000.

This means that the manager must lose money for his own account in order to earn money for his investors.

The management of ABC decides to go to a 60-40 sharing arrangement with an exclusion for acreage investments in Canada. A study of their 10 years of operations shows that 40% is a reasonable figure, so problem (a) is under control. While ABC Oil dislikes investing in tangibles, a computer study shows that the approach is profitable to the company, so (b) is not a concern. The problem in (c) is overcome by excluding Canadian acreage. The problem in (d) is attacked by a thorough disclosure section in the prospectus.

8. *Liquidity*

It would be helpful to investors if their limited partnership interests could be sold easily. There is no question that a redemption feature would facilitate sales of program interests. For that reason, the sales people feel that a surrender feature should be incorporated into the program.

In this area, however, the management of the program decides not to allow possible increased sales to influence their decision on program

154

structure. The decision not to have a surrender feature is based on several factors:

a) The lack of resources within ABC Oil Company to purchase redeemed units if more than a fairly small amount are surrendered;

b) The intention to convert the partnership interests into corporate form in a few years.

9. *Conflict of interest*

The possibility is raised that ABC might want to provide property and services to the oil programs under its management. In particular, it could turnkey wells to the program.

While there is merit to turnkeying wells in some areas, the management decides not to do so. The reasoning is that the agency relationship between manager and investor ought to preclude any "self-dealing."

II. *The Marketing Phase*

About 4 months after filing with the SEC, ABC's oil program becomes effective. Upon the advice of the sales force, program interests are qualified for sale in 30 states.

It soon became apparent that oil program interests are more difficult to sell than anyone had anticipated. The objective of $1,250,000 for the April 1 partnership looks very difficult. While dealer interest is good, sales just aren't as high as they were predicted. With a lot of effort from the wholesalers and a trip to a number of brokerage offices by the President of ABC, $750,000 is finally raised for the partnership.

While $750,000 is a good performance for any oil program's first partnership, ABC has a problem. In order to control some high quality prospects, the company had committed to $500,000 in exploratory projects and put them in inventory prior to closing the program. At the time of those commitments, the management of ABC had expected a $1,250,000 program with a budget for exploration of over $600,000. At $750,000, the program's exploration budget is only $394,500 (including exploratory overhead). Further, about 50% of the $500,000 allocation is in Louisiana—which means that Louisiana is getting too much of the partnership's exploration money.

ABC's management has to do some quick shuffling. Rather than drop the projects, it manages to delay some of the wells long enough to allow participation by the program that closes on July 1. It also defers commitments that it was about to make for the July program.

III. *The Exploration Phase*

With a $750,000 program, the following budget is constructed:

Program Size	$750,000
Commissions (8%)	60,000
Registration Costs (1.0%)	7,500
ABC Exploratory Overhead	75,000
ABC Management Overhead	75,000

Funds available for Exploration
    and Development   532,500
Exploration Budget (60%)   319,500
Development Budget (40%)   213,000

The exploration budget is allocated to 16 prospects. Seven are in south Louisiana, five in Texas, and four in central Alberta. In 12 of the 16 prospects, the original geology was done by ABC. The remaining four were submitted by others.

The average working interest taken by the program is 25%. In most of the prospects, later limited partnerships take a share. Other oil companies also participate in the projects with ABC Oil.

Four of the prospects are rank wildcats. While their chances of success are not great, the potential rewards are excellent. The remaining 12 are less risky. As a group they have an average probability of success of about 20%.

By February of the following year, all 16 wells have been drilled. The results are:

1. 14 dry holes;
2. 1 marginal oil well in Texas (33⅓% working interest);
3. 1 good gas well in Louisiana (25% working interest);
4. 1 dry hole in Alberta on a good acreage position. Testing of the well prior to abandonment strongly suggests that a thick, porous gas reservoir may exist to the northeast. (25% working interest)

IV. *The Development Stage*

A development budget of $213,000 is available to pursue the successes during the exploratory phase. This creates a problem because it does not appear to be adequate. The following money seems to be needed:

1. Texas oil well—$40,000 for a 33⅓% interest in two more wells:
2. Louisiana gas well—$120,000 for a 25% interest in four more wells:
3. Alberta acreage—$35,000 to buy more land from the crown and $40,000 for a 25% interest in another well to the northeast.

The total funds required amount to $235,000—$22,000 more than is available. Since the Louisiana property has the most promise, it will be drilled first. The shortage in development money is small, so it will be covered by production income in the Louisiana gas properties.

A dispute arises within the management of ABC Oil as to whether additional program money should be expended in Alberta. The issue turns upon whether the information gained in the initial dry hole is sufficiently promising to justify expenditure of development money in the project. Part of the management feels that the prospect is still exploratory even though the risk has been reduced. The other part believes that the next well has a 50% chance of success with high potential rewards.

A decision is made to acquire additional land and drill a well. Since the program appears to be successful with its Louisiana and Texas properties, the downside risk is not terribly great while the potential is excellent.

Within another 12 months, the development stage is completed. The results are:

1. 1 dry hole and 1 producer in Texas;
2. 1 dry hole and 3 producers in Louisiana;
3. 1 dry hole in Alberta that reduces the potential size of the reservoir, but does not merit dropping the acreage.

V. *The Writeoff*

By the end of the first year, 14 of the 16 exploratory wells had been drilled. About 40% of the development work had also been done by year end. As a result, an 80% writeoff is created in the first year. Additional drilling in the second year is partially offset by production income, but deductions still amount to another 15%.

VI. *Measuring the Results*

An engineering evaluation is done on the program's properties by an independent firm about 2 years after the program is organized. Prior to that time, investors in the program had frequently asked for value estimates from ABC Oil. Management felt that a 2-year period was the minimum time necessary to provide meaningful figures. This is so because:

1. The Texas and Louisiana production needs about 1 year of history to formulate reasonable reserve estimates;
2. Other oil companies have been drilling on land adjacent to the partnership's land in Alberta. That drilling would materially affect the value of the partnership's investment in the area.

The evaluation by an independent engineering firm shows:

Value of Texas properties to a 33⅓ % working interest	
(future net income discounted to present value at 7%)	$170,000
Value of Louisiana properties to a 25% working interest	
(future net income discounted to present value at 7%)	450,000
Value of Alberta acreage	100,000
Total present value	$720,000
Original investment	750,000
Ratio of total present value to original investment	96%

VII. *Liquidity*

By the end of the second full year after the formation of the partnership, it becomes clear that a limited partnership arrangement is no longer an advantage. Instead of allowing the flow through of tax losses, the partnership is showing taxable income. Furthermore, the limited partnership interests have no market, and some investors have expressed a desire to sell their interests.

The best answer is to exchange the partnership interests for common stock in a corporation. Common stock is a more liquid security that will stop the flow-through of taxable income. Since three other partnerships managed by ABC Oil are in a similar position, the four partnerships will be exchanged together. Total present value of the partnerships is about $3.5 million.

There are several ways in which to approach an exchange:

1. Exchange partnership interests for common stock in the management company, ABC Oil;

2. Exchange partnership interests for common stock in a newly created corporation whose purpose it is to take over all the assets of the partnerships;

3. Sell the partnerships to an established oil company for stock;

4. Create a corporation which will acquire the partnership interests as well as a small oil company with established management.

The first approach is discarded for two reasons. ABC Oil Company is a privately held organization, and its stockholders want it to remain that way. Beyond that, IRS rules require that the limited partners own 80% or more of the corporation that results from the exchange. If they do not, the exchange is taxable. A taxable exchange may cause problems for the investor if he is not sent the money to pay the tax. Neither ABC Oil nor the partnerships have adequate cash for that purpose.

The second approach (creating a new corporation) would have merit only if the company formed were considerably larger than $3.5 million. The management of ABC Oil is not willing to leave ABC to run the new company. Starting a management group from the ground floor is both difficult and dangerous.

Several oil companies express an interest in buying out the partnerships. They indicate that they can solve the taxable exchange problem by paying part cash and part stock. Unfortunately, no agreement can be reached on a price and the discussions are terminated.

It is finally decided to create a new corporation which will also buy a small oil company in Houston. Since the value of that company is only $750,000, no tax will be created in the exchange. The company is fairly new, but its management has an excellent reputation and is capable of doing a fine job of running the corporation.